The Social Organization of Honeybees

John B. Free
M.A., Ph.D., D.Sc., F.I.Biol.
Rothamsted Experimental Station, Harpenden

© J.B. Free 1977

First Published 1977
by Edward Arnold (Publishers) Limited

ISBN 0-907908-65-9

Reprinted 1980
Reprinted by Northern Bee Books 1993

All rights reserved. No part of this publication may be reproduced, stored in a retrieval system, or transmitted, in any form or by any means, electronic, mechanical, photocopying, recording or otherwise, without the permission of Edward Arnold (Publishers) Limited and in the case of the 1993 reprint, Northern Bee Books.

For my Sons

Printed by Arc & Throstle Press, Todmorden

This edition published by Northern Bee Books, Scout Bottom Farm, Mytholmroyd, Hebden Bridge HX7 5JS

General Preface to the Series

It is no longer possible for one textbook to cover the whole field of Biology and to remain sufficiently up to date. At the same time teachers and students at school, college or university need to keep abreast of recent trends and know where the most significant developments are taking place.

To meet the need for this progressive approach the Institute of Biology has for some years sponsored this series of booklets dealing with subjects specially selected by a panel of editors. The enthusiastic acceptance of the series by teachers and students at school, college and university shows the usefulness of the books in providing a clear and up-to-date coverage of topics, particularly in areas of research and changing views.

Among features of the series are the attention given to methods, the inclusion of a selected list of books for further reading and, wherever possible, suggestions for practical work.

Reader's comments will be welcomed by the author or the Education Officer of the Institute.

1977

The Institute of Biology,
41 Queen's Gate,
London, SW7 5HU

Preface

In spite of the readiness with which it defends its nest, the honeybee has long been favoured by man because of the honey and wax it produces, and recently it has been increasingly used to pollinate agricultural and horticultural crops. However, the honeybee's conspicuous social organization and the altruistic and apparently complex behaviour displayed by individuals have undoubtedly been the main reasons why it has received so much attention, with the result that there is a greater volume of literature on the honeybee than on any other insect.

Recent research, by many ethologists, physiologists and biochemists, has concentrated on discovering how the activities of many individuals within the honeybee colony are controlled and co-ordinated so that the behaviour of the colony as a whole is adapted to its constantly changing environment. The findings have often been both surprising and far reaching in their implications, and have stimulated fruitful studies on many other insects.

1977

J. B. F.

Contents

	Preface	iii
1	The Organization and Structure of the Colony	1
	1.1 Introduction 1.2 Female castes 1.3 Duties of workers 1.4 Use of comb for food storage and brood rearing	
2	Regulation of Colony Activities	13
	2.1 Introduction 2.2 Seasonal growth 2.3 Temperature regulation 2.4 Co-ordination of activities and communication within the nest	
3	Colony Defence	30
	3.1 Introduction 3.2 Defensive mechanisms 3.3 Aggressiveness 3.4 Guard Bees 3.5 Recognition of intruders	
4	Collection of Forage	37
	4.1 Factors determining type of forage collected 4.2 Attractiveness of forage 4.3 Dance language	
5	Queen and Worker Production	48
	5.1 Development and caste determination 5.2 Queen replacement 5.3 Workers' ovary development	
6	Colony Reproduction	54
	6.1 Swarming 6.2 Drone production 6.3 Mating	
7	Conclusions	67
	Further Reading	68

1 The Organization and Structure of the Honeybee Colony

1.1 Introduction

The honeybee colony is one of the most striking achievements of evolution. There are four species of honeybee. The most widely distributed species (*Apis mellifera*) has become adapted to flourish in a large area of the earth's surface and occurs in the tropics and sub-arctic as well as throughout the temperate zone. The other three species are confined to South-eastern Asia. *Apis florea* and *Apis dorsata* nest in the open and each colony builds its single comb under the branch of a tree or overhang of rock. *Apis cerana*, like *A. mellifera*, nests in enclosed dark spaces such as rock cavities and hollow trees and each colony builds several parallel combs. The anatomy and social organization of *Apis cerana* also appears to be similar to that of *A. mellifera*. However, much more is known about *A. mellifera* than the other honeybees, and unless otherwise stated the following account refers to findings about this species.

At all times of the year a honeybee colony contains a fertile female, the 'queen' (Fig. 1–1), and numerous infertile females, the 'workers'. It also contains developing brood for most of the year, and male, or 'drone', bees (Fig. 1–2) for most of the spring and summer.

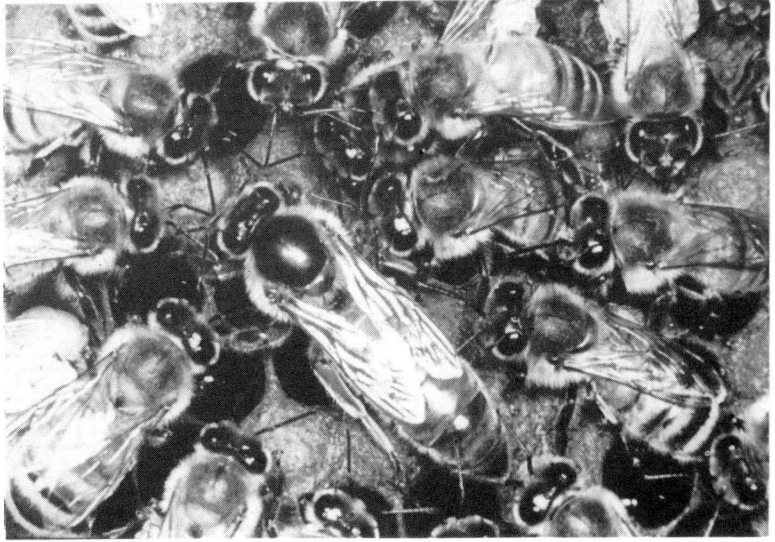

Fig. 1–1   Queen honeybee surrounded by attendant workers.

Fig. 1–2 Part of a comb with a drone and workers.

1.2 Female castes

Differences in the anatomy, physiology and behaviour of a worker and queen are associated with the specialization of the queen for egg-laying to the exclusion of many other activities and result in a clear cut division of labour between them. The queen is larger than a worker, has a proportionally larger abdomen containing 300 or more ovarioles, has a higher metabolic rate enabling her to lay 1000 or more eggs per day and has a greater longevity. However, she has a less complicated behavioural repertoire and a smaller brain than workers, her body lacks the plumose pollen-gathering hairs of the worker and the pollen-gathering apparatus, or corbiculae, on the worker's rear legs; she lacks the wax glands and hypopharyngeal glands of the worker but has larger mandibular glands (Fig. 1–3). In association with its sterility, a worker has few ovarioles, usually undeveloped, and cannot mate.

1.3 Duties of workers

Queen honeybees are specialized for egg-laying; all other tasks are performed by morphologically identical workers. During the middle of the summer when workers live four to six weeks, approximately the first two to three weeks is spent in nest work and the remainder in foraging.

Many observers have recorded the activities of marked worker bees of different ages and have found that individuals do not specialize in

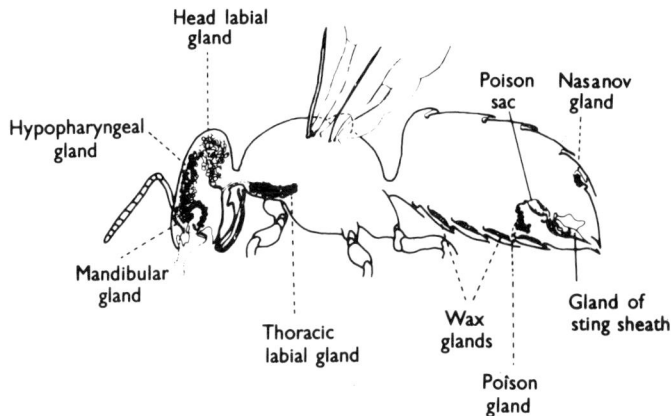

Fig. 1-3 Glands of the female honeybee in cross-section. The mandibular glands and glands in the sting chamber of the worker honeybee produce alarm pheromones. The hypopharyngeal and mandibular glands of workers produce brood food. Substances from the head and thoracic labial glands of workers are used in grooming, cleaning and feeding. Secretions from the wax glands of workers are used for building comb. Pheromones from the Nasanov gland of workers attract other workers. Pheromones from the mandibular glands of the queen attract drones and inhibit queen rearing. Queens have no hypopharyngeal glands, wax glands or Nasanov glands. (After Ribbands, C. R., 1953, *The Behaviour and Social Life of Honeybees*, London, Bee Research Association.)

particular tasks, but that each does a variety of tasks, the preferred task tending to change as it grows older (Figs. 1–4 and 1–5). In general, with increase in age bees undertake four overlapping series of tasks as follows:

(a) Cell cleaning
(b) Feeding larvae, comb building
(c) Comb building; nectar reception; pollen packing; cell cleaning; removing debris; guarding
(d) Foraging

The glandular systems of a bee that are associated with producing brood food and wax, develop and retrogress in association with changes in its preference for the various tasks within the nest. For much of this time bees in the nest may seem idle, often for hours at a time, but such resting bees may, in fact, be secreting wax or brood food.

However, there is much variation in the age at which bees undertake various tasks in the nest and at which they begin foraging. Bees that forage early in their lives may abbreviate or omit some tasks in the nest.

1.3.1 Cleaning activities

A newly emerged bee first cleans itself and when a few hours old begins

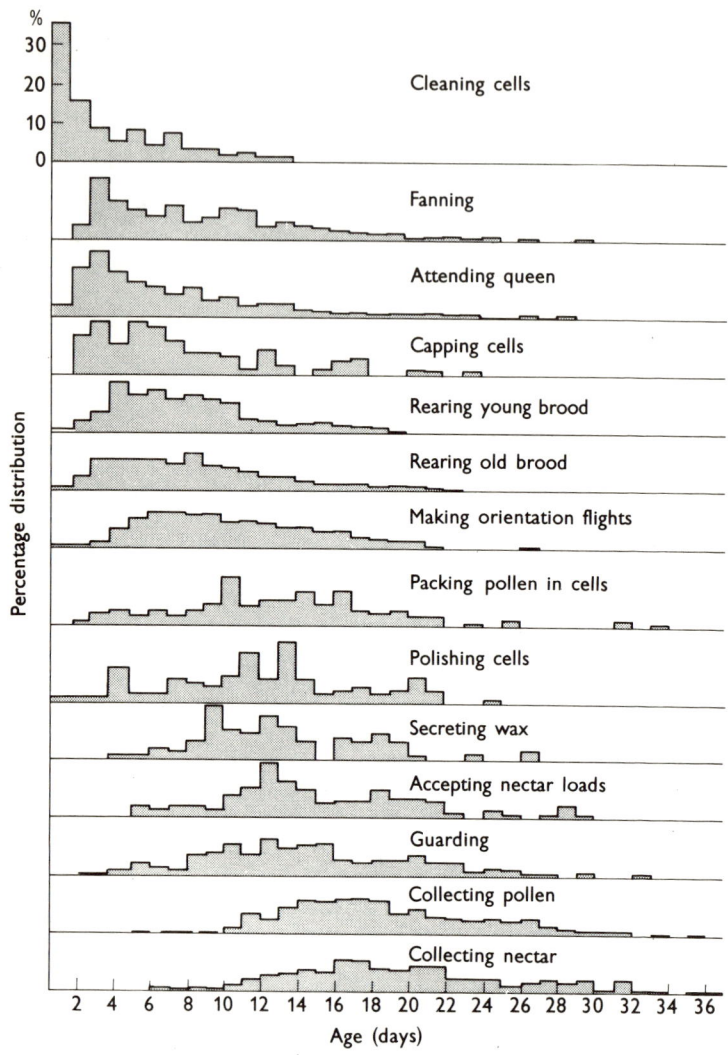

Fig. 1–4 Percentage age distribution of bees engaged in different activities. (From Sakagami, S. F., 1953, *Japanese Journal of Zoology*, **11**, 117–85.)

cleaning cells that have contained brood. The ragged edges of capping are ignored by these young cell-cleaners but are removed by older bees (4 to 20 days old). As well as cleaning cells bees fly from the hive carrying debris such as old capping, dead brood and mouldy pollen; this work is usually done by bees just prior to foraging. Bees of any age that are engaged in nest work frequently clean each other and the drones. A bee

§ 1.3

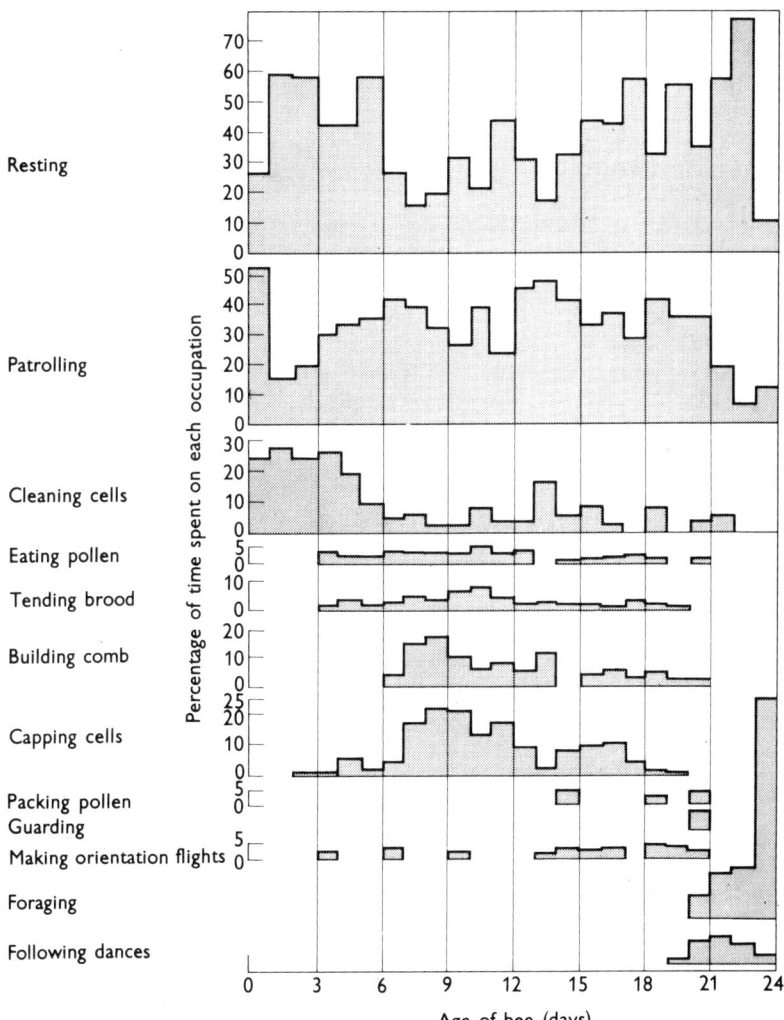

Fig. 1–5 The percentage of time a single worker bee spent on various activities during the first 24 days of its life. (From Ribbands, C. R., 1953, 'The behaviour and social life of honeybees,' London, Bee Research Association, after Lindauer, M., 1952, *Z. vergl. Physiol.*, **34**, 299–345.)

waiting to be cleaned performs a grooming invitation dance during which it rapidly stamps its legs and shakes its body from side to side. This usually results in a nearby bee cleaning it, particularly in the wing bases and in the constriction between the thorax and abdomen where a bee is unable to clean itself.

1.3.2 Brood feeding

Larvae are given food which comes mostly from the hypopharyngeal and mandibular glands of worker bees, although secretions from the post-cerebral and thoracic glands may be added (Fig. 1–3). The hypopharyngeal glands become fully developed in worker bees of three days old and remain so for the next two weeks or so during which time the bees are able to feed larvae.

The larvae receive intensive care. An individual larva is inspected by bees between a total of one to two thousand times, and following about a tenth of these inspections the bee concerned deposits food on the cell base or the cell wall, near to the larva's mouth.

A bee's brood food glands cannot supply food continuously and a bee spends very little of its time actually feeding larvae; so it is to be expected that bees engaged in feeding brood would also be active in other ways.

1.3.3 Building comb

Wax is used to build new comb, repair old comb, and to cover over ('cap') cells containing pupae or ripe honey. Bees producing wax tend to cluster in parts of the colony where wax is needed in abundance. The wax issues as thin scales from four pairs of glands opening on the ventral surface of the abdomen (Fig. 1–3). These wax glands are fully developed in bees from about one to three weeks old, although younger and older bees can also produce wax. The wax scales from the glands are transferred by the back legs to the mandibles and forelegs, where they are manipulated and added to the comb.

In building new comb the actions of hundreds of individuals are integrated and co-ordinated, but the individual bees that are building cells do not always appear to co-operate, and a bee sometimes removes the wax recently added by another and puts it elsewhere; a bee in need of wax obviously must not go too far from the cell it is building, otherwise it will not find it again.

During their last days of nest duty, bees receive nectar from foragers and smooth down pollen loads in cells. When there is abundant incoming forage and storage combs are filled to capacity, the nectar receivers sometimes have difficulty in getting rid of their loads and the receiving bees are fully occupied. Possibly, under such circumstances, the nectar loads the bees are forced to store in their honeystomachs are automatically assimilated and converted to wax, which is used to build additional storage combs and so help relieve the nectar congestion.

1.3.4 Orientation flights

When a bee flies for the first time it orientates itself to its nest's position while making increasingly wider circles in the air; on successive trips bees go further afield but even on long flights, may not collect food and will solicit it from others on their return. These orientation flights first occur when bees are three to seventeen days old, and tend to be on windless sunny days between 10.00 and 16.00 h. Accumulation of faeces together with increased phototropic responses probably initiate orientation flights.

1.3.5 Foraging

The age at which bees first forage differs greatly (usually when they are between 10 and 30 days old) and in general, the earlier bees make orientation flights, the earlier they first forage. The hypopharyngeal glands of foragers soon degenerate, even when the foragers are relatively young. Although there is little variation in size of honeybee workers (about 80–110 mg in weight) the larger ones are likely to forage at an earlier age than the smaller.

Foragers collect nectar, pollen or less commonly propolis (resin obtained from plant buds), and water (see also Chapter 4). The pollen and propolis are carried in the corbiculae and the nectar and water in the crop (honeystomach). There is no sequence of foraging duties with age, and most bees collect nectar and pollen sometime during their lives.

1.3.6 Adaptability

Colonies do not always undergo the regular sequence of brood rearing and colony growth typical of large undisturbed colonies in summer, and the proportion of brood to bees may be subject to considerable fluctuations.

Thus during poor foraging weather brood rearing may decrease, eventually resulting in an increased ratio of old to new bees. During orientation flights, a large proportion of bees may inadvertently stray into colonies other than their own and, because of their position, some colonies are likely to gain bees at the expense of others. The regular balance of bees and brood is also disturbed when a colony swarms, and the swarm itself may not produce any brood for several days. Brood rearing ceases for much of the winter and all the bees present in the early spring when brood rearing begins are several months old; in these circumstances the oldest bees tend to forage, and the youngest bees, that did not feed brood in the autumn, do tasks in the nest.

Bees are evidently able to adjust themselves to changed conditions, and several investigations have been attempted to find how adaptable they are. Some investigators have initiated colonies by putting together newly-emerged workers and a queen either with empty combs, or with combs containing brood, and it was found that very young bees, sometimes only four days old, foraged even though they had fully developed hypopharyngeal glands. Other observers have formed colonies of combs containing larvae, a queen and foraging bees only. Soon, the hypopharyngeal glands of many of these older bees had redeveloped and the brood was being adequately fed, while the hypopharyngeal glands of bees that continued foraging remained atrophied. Similar experiments have shown that older bees can redevelop their wax glands and build comb in response to the need for more brood rearing and food storage space.

It is therefore apparent that the task that needs doing can determine the condition of a worker's glands. However, the converse also appears to be true. Thus anaesthetizing bees with carbon dioxide causes their hypopharyngeal glands to retrogress sooner than usual and such bees also forage earlier than usual. When new bees are kept for a week on a diet of carbohydrate their hypopharyngeal glands never develop and they forage earlier than usual, omitting the task of brood feeding. Both these examples demonstrate that the state of the development of a bee's glands can greatly influence its occupation.

1.3.7 Mechanism of allocation of duties

In an undisturbed colony the brood is on the central combs; on either side and sometimes above and below as well there are probably combs containing only stores of honey and pollen. Very young bees are found almost exclusively on the brood combs, but with increase in their age more bees occur on the storage combs.

The temperature in the centre of the brood nest is about 35°C and decreases toward the periphery of the colony. With advancing age a bee's metabolic rate increases and its preferred temperature decreases which partly explains the tendency of bees to cluster at the periphery of the colony as they grow older. Once at the periphery they become conditioned to the lower temperature there, so that their dislike of the brood nest temperature is further increased, and their greater ability than younger bees to survive cold and probably remain active and fly at low temperatures is further reinforced.

Young bees prefer the darkness of the nest, but as they become older they also become photopositive; this is another physiological factor influencing their preference for the periphery of the nest and their urge to forage outside it. Because bees engaged in nest work tend to be at the hub of their colony's activities, they may learn their colony's requirements through direct individual experience. They frequently wander about the nest, inspecting cells and brood, and while doing so each bee probably gathers for itself information about the tasks needing attention. Presumably the stimuli encountered initiate the appropriate activity response in physiologically and behaviourally suitable bees.

Possibly these inspection visits also serve to stimulate gland development; thus the presence of empty space in the nest suitable for comb building stimulates more bees to develop their wax glands, and the presence of brood is necessary to stimulate bees to develop their hypopharyngeal glands fully. Because there must be considerable variation in the number and types of stimuli received by different bees, individual variations in the time schedule of activities are to be expected.

Bees will continue with a particular task as long as is necessary, but under normal conditions in summer, the regular production of worker bees ensures a continuous flow of new recruits to each occupation and it seems that the presence of sufficient or a superabundance of workers at any task leads to the promotion of the older bees to the next stage; for example lack of work inside the nest may cause bees to forage when they are approaching normal foraging age, or when they have already done nest duties for some time.

When the amount of incoming nectar is decreased, and the older nest-bees have increased numbers of bees begging from them, it is easy to envisage how they are inclined to follow recruiting dances of successful foragers in their vicinity and to become foragers themselves.

1.4 Use of comb for food storage and brood rearing

The cells in the combs of a honeybee are hexagonal in cross-section and are of two basic types. The larger deeper cells are used for the rearing of drone brood and the smaller cells for the rearing of worker brood (page 59). Irregularly shaped cells are constructed where worker and drone cells adjoin and where combs are attached to their supports. Cells slope slightly downwards toward the mid-rib of the comb.

The same cell may be used at different times for food storage and brood rearing. Cells for honey storage may be extended to twice the depth of cells used for brood. When new, cells consist entirely of wax (white in colour) secreted by worker bees, but after brood has been reared in them they are lined with cocoons and accumulate larval faeces in their bases. Cocoons are light brown, so that after repeated use for brood rearing, combs become dark brown or even black. Combs not used for brood rearing remain white or become yellowish by absorbing coloured substances from pollen.

All species of honeybee collect nectar and pollen in excess of the immediate needs of their colony and store it in the combs. The food they hoard enables them to survive periods of dearth in the tropics and periods of cold in temperate climates. Although since ancient times man has exploited the tendency of honeybees to hoard food, the factors influencing hoarding have only recently been studied.

1.4.1 Food storage in honeystomachs

Bees store nectar and honey in their honeystomachs as well as in their comb. The tendency to do so differs with their present occupation and past experience.

Although in general, worker bees about to give food have fuller honeystomachs than those about to receive it (page 26), there is a considerable overlap in the amounts of food in the honeystomachs of bees of these two categories, and whether a bee offers or begs for food is certainly not governed entirely by the amount it possesses.

When performing duties such as larval feeding or wax secretion a bee normally retains more food in its honeystomach than when occupied with other tasks. The particular environment a bee occupies within the hive may also have an effect on the amount of food retained in the honeystomach. Thus bees on the outside of a winter cluster (page 20) contain more food in their honeystomachs and probably consume more than those in the centre. An improvement or deterioration in the attractiveness and quality of food provided also influences the amount bees retain in their honeystomachs, and even brief periods of food deprivation or exposure to cold greatly increases food retention.

When groups of honeybees are confined to a cage without any comb they tend to store food in their honeystomachs thus reflecting the similar behaviour of swarming bees or bees whose colonies have been disturbed by smoke (i.e. bees that have become or are likely to become separated from their comb). The amount of honey or nectar that caged bees store in combs also varies genetically, with the environmental temperature, with the ages of the bees concerned and with their previous physiological and behavioural experience including food deprivation and length of confinement.

Darkness and the presence of a queen encourage bees to store food in combs, but the presence of light and absence of a queen encourage bees to store in their honeystomach even when a comb is present.

1.4.2 Factors deciding a cell's use

A cell's function seems to be determined to a great extent by its position in relation to the natural arrangement of brood and food stores in the nest or hive.

During most of the year brood is reared in the lower part of the central combs of a natural nest, which consists of a few large combs, or in the central combs in the lower part of a hive. In such a comb in a hive the brood often occupies a semi-circular area, the top two corners of the comb and bands of cells at the side edges being used for storing nectar and pollen. Combs above the brood area and on either side of it are usually either empty or contain stores of honey and pollen, the pollen usually being concentrated near the brood combs.

However, cells are also preferred for different functions according to their structure and previous use. This has been shown in a series of experiments in which small sections of empty combs of different types, or which had been used by bees for different purposes, were arranged in a checkerbrood pattern and the use bees made of them was compared.

Bees prefer to store honey in worker rather than drone cells, and they store little or no pollen in drone combs. The reason is obscure, but leaves

§ 1.4 USE OF COMB FOR FOOD STORAGE AND BROOD REARING 11

the drone cells free to receive brood at the appropriate time of the year (page 58).

Egg-laying (Fig. 1–7) and brood rearing occurs as readily in new worker comb as in comb in which brood has already been reared, but less readily in comb used for food storage. It seems probable that cells receiving eggs are scent marked in some way by the queen and workers. Combs in which eggs have been laid or brood has been reared is subsequently favoured for storing nectar or pollen.

Because new cells are selected as readily as vacated brood cells for brood rearing, but vacated brood cells are favoured for food storage, and because once a cell has been used for food storage it is disfavoured for brood rearing, it follows that in a 'wild' colony proportionately more of the newly produced combs than the old comb is used for brood rearing. Hence, there must be a tendency for old combs formerly in the brood nest to be used for storing food, and for brood rearing to be pushed onto recently built combs (Fig. 1–6).

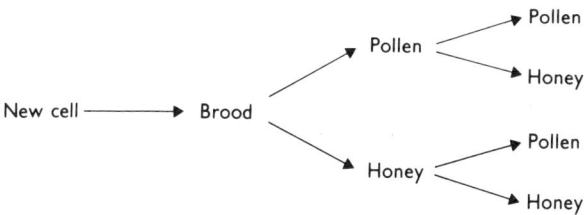

Fig. 1–6   Progressive use of cells in a natural honeybee colony. (After Free, J. B. and Williams, Ingrid H., 1975, *J. Ent.* (A), 47–62.)

Progressive removal of the brood nest on to new comb is advantageous because the bases of cells in which several generations of brood have been reared contain an accumulation of cocoons and larval faeces, so that the space available for rearing the larvae progressively diminishes and ultimately the bees produced are smaller than usual. [Although it is not known how small a cell has to become before it is no longer suitable for brood rearing, presumably natural selection has produced worker bees of optimum size and any size diminution is disadvantageous.] However, modern beekeeping practices often frustrate the bees' natural inclination to store food in the old brood area of the nest and to transfer brood rearing activities to the newer combs. In these circumstances the influence of the immediate past history of a cell on its future use is considerably lessened, and its location in the colony in relation to the brood nest and stores assumes even greater importance.

Although empty worker cells are cleaned by workers before re-use, and this cell cleaning is encouraged by the presence of the queen, the bees do not appear to prepare them for any particular function. However, it is probable that the number of eggs a queen can lay is determined by the number of cells the bees have cleaned in the brood nest of the colony, and that the amount of pollen collected depends on the number of empty clean cells at the periphery of the brood combs and on combs adjacent to them (page 40).

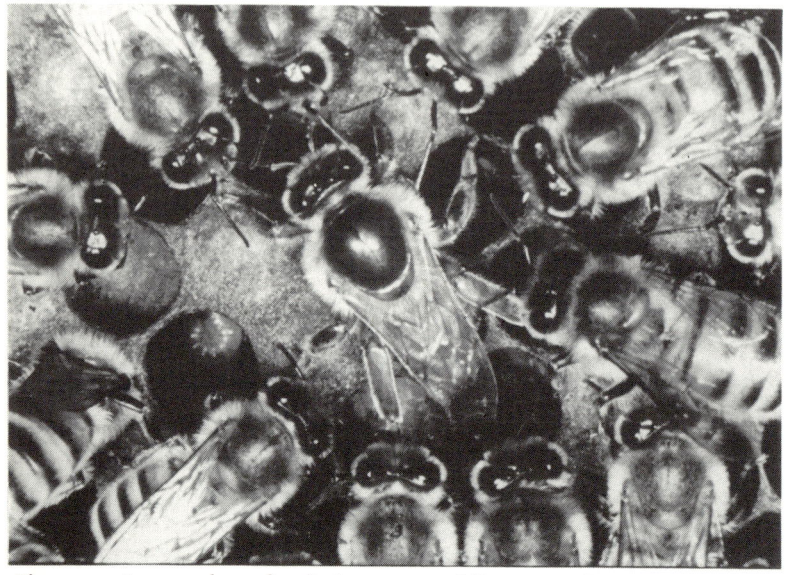

Fig. 1–7   A queen honeybee laying an egg while surrounded by her attendant workers.

2 Regulation of Colony Activities

2.1 Introduction

The successful distribution of the honeybee owes much to the colony's ability to adjust to seasonal changes and to exert considerable control over its internal physical environment. During periods of dearth when it cannot forage, the colony can survive on food stored in its comb. In such conditions little brood is present and the colony may consist of a cluster of the queen and workers only. However, with the advent of a more favourable season, more brood is reared, the number of worker bees increases, drone rearing begins, new queens may be reared and the colony may reproduce itself by swarming.

2.2 Seasonal growth

In temperate climates most of the bees present in early spring are old overwintered bees and the size of a colony is directly related to its size the previous autumn. These old bees have a low life expectancy and most will survive only a few days of continuous foraging, although a few that were reared in late autumn may live until early June. Indeed, in early spring, more bees die than emerge, so the colony decreases to its minimum size for the year (Fig. 2-1); but this size decrease is only temporary, and soon sufficient worker bees are being reared for the population to expand.

There is little nectar or pollen available for a colony to collect early in the year, but as more plants come into flower, more forage becomes available. Coinciding with this the colony has a larger proportion of young bees which have a greater life expectancy, so more foragers are available to collect the increased amount of forage.

In response to changes in the quantity of forage entering their nest the bees regulate the number of brood reared. This especially applies to changes in the quantity of pollen collected, which is the sole source of protein for the bees. Bees can influence the rate at which a queen lays eggs by the number of cells cleaned and prepared to receive them, and they can control the supply of food they give to the queen and hence her ability to produce eggs. However, although the egg-laying rate of a queen can be greatly influenced by the bees in her colony, she is able to maintain her egg-laying rate, to some extent, independent of them and this must help to smooth out the effects of small fluctuations in forage income on brood production.

Workers also control the number of larvae being reared by eating some or all of them. Following the winter break in brood rearing, eggs are

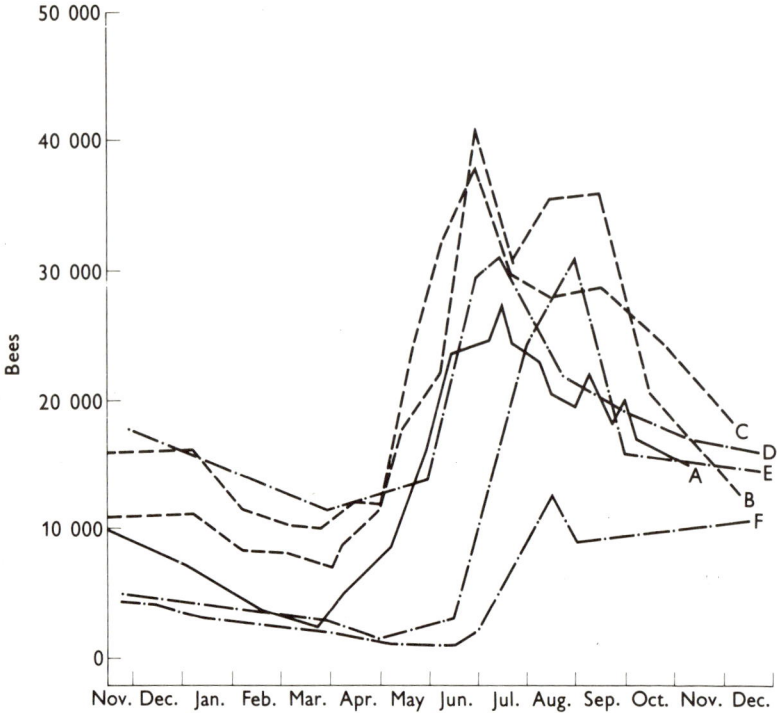

Fig. 2-1 The adult bee population throughout the year in one colony (A) in 1945 (———) in two colonies (B and C) in 1946 (– – – –) and in three colonies (D, E and F) in 1947 (·–·–). (From Jeffree, E. P., 1955, *J. econ. Ent.*, **48**, 723–6.)

sometimes laid several weeks before brood is actually reared. An increase in egg-laying may follow an improvement in forage supply that proves to have been temporary, and, by eating some of the eggs or young larvae, the workers can adjust the amount of brood being reared to the current supply of forage.

As a result of the increased brood rearing that follows increased foraging in the spring, the adult bee population increases, and provided forage remains abundant, so also does the number of foragers and amount of forage collected. In turn, the amount of forage collected is influenced by the quantity of brood present (Fig. 2-2). Both these factors are dependent on colony size; in the spring small colonies rear proportionally more brood per bee than large ones (Fig. 2-3) and the bees of small colonies forage proportionally more than those of large ones.

Increased colony growth enables a queen to reach her maximum rate of egg-laying, which may be about 1500 eggs per day, and which is

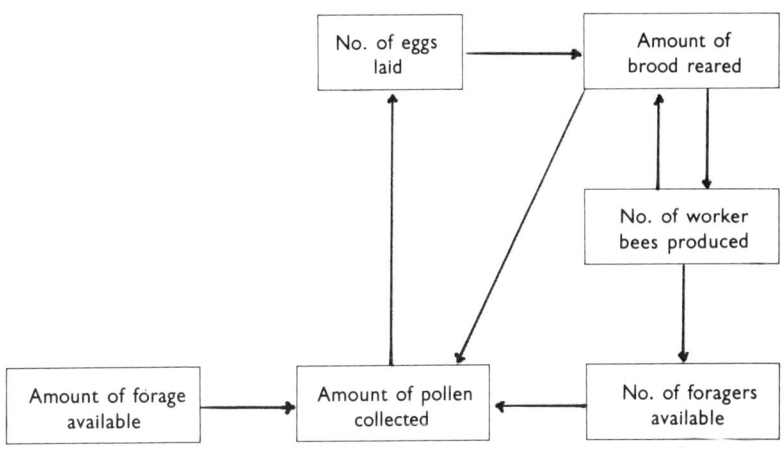

Fig. 2–2 Factors determining the amount of pollen collected by a honeybee colony.

determined partly by the behaviour of her workers and partly by her own limitations. When the queen attains her peak of egg-laying, usually near mid-summer, the proportion of adult bees to brood increases, so there are more bees foraging and proportionally fewer larvae to feed. This is why mature colonies store a greater surplus of food than those which are still growing. Different colonies may vary considerably in their size when mature, and the amounts of honey stored by mature colonies of different sizes are directly proportional to their populations.

Although mere day-to-day fluctuations in the amount of forage collected probably influence brood rearing little, larger fluctuations may have a considerable effect. However, any decrease in brood rearing and subsequently in the number of adults produced is compensated to some extent by the increased longevity of the bees. While the longevity of bees is greatest when there is least brood, it is least when there is most brood and decreases in accordance with their date of emergence from early spring to mid-summer and then increases again (Fig. 2–4).

Foraging is more arduous and more hazardous than nest duty and affects longevity more. The decreased longevity in mid-summer is probably caused by increased foraging rather than increased brood-rearing, as colonies tend to reach their maximum size at this time, so that the brood/worker ratio decreases and bees begin to forage at an earlier age.

In late summer and autumn a decrease in available forage has the direct effect of increasing longevity and decreasing brood rearing, although the latter will also favour increased longevity. However, other factors may have an important influence because small colonies continue brood

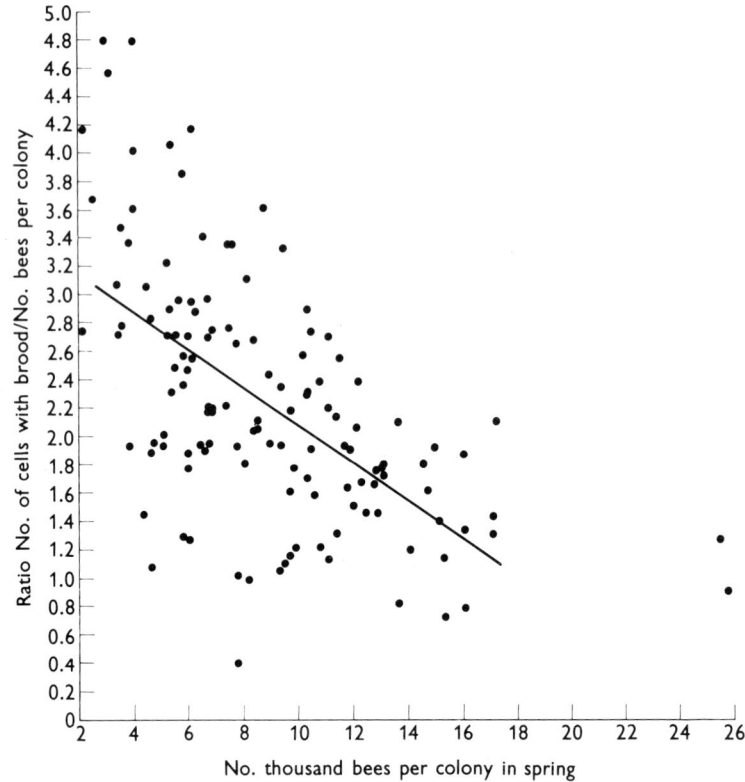

Fig. 2–3 The relationship between the number of bees and the ratio of brood/bees in colonies in the spring. (From Free, J. B. and Racey, P. A., 1968, *Ent. exp. & appl.*, **11**, 241–9.)

rearing later in the autumn than large colonies, and colonies with young queens rear brood later in the autumn than colonies with old queens.

The increased longevity associated with lack of work is insufficient to compensate for decreased brood rearing, and the greatly increased longevity of bees that overwinter is dependent on differences in the physiology of 'winter' and 'summer' bees. During the winter most bees have well developed hypopharyngeal glands and 'fat bodies' which contain protein as well as fat; bees with the life expectancy of 'winter' bees can be produced by feeding abundant pollen to young bees in the summer. As a result of their physiological resources and diminished activity, many of the bees that emerge in August, September and October survive the winter.

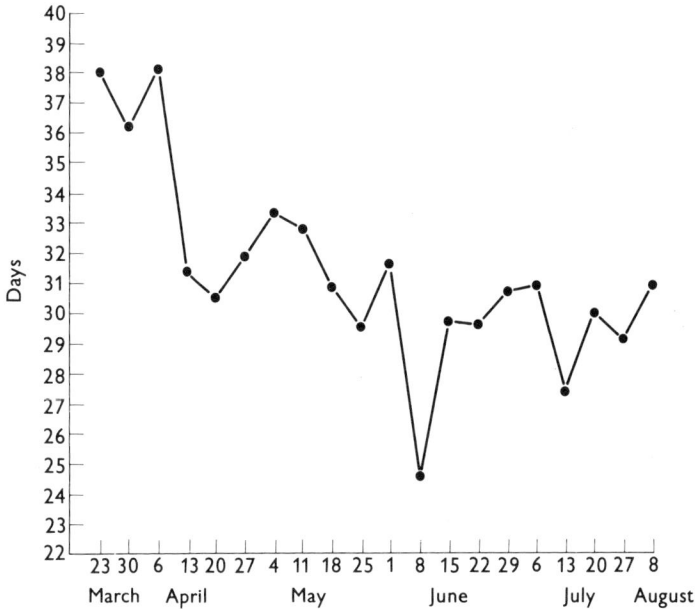

Fig. 2–4 The average longevity of worker bees that emerged at various times during spring and summer. (After: Free, J. B. and Spencer-Booth, Yvette, 1959. *Proc. Roy. Ent. Soc. London*, (A), **34**, 141–50.)

2.3 Temperature regulation

Bees are attracted to each other by sight, vibration, heat and odour and form a cluster within their nest or hive. The minimum number of bees necessary to form a cluster diminishes with decrease in temperature, but at 20°C a cluster does not form unless 50 or more bees are present. Within the isolated microclimate of the cluster they build their waxen combs, rear brood and store food, and are able to regulate its temperature and humidity and so avoid conditions in which individual bees would die.

2.3.1 Response to high temperature

Bees and brood produce metabolic heat, and the brood area of a honeybee colony is usually kept at 34 to 35°C and is allowed to fluctuate little in parts where eggs or young larvae are present. At temperatures a few degrees above this isolated bees live longer in humid than in dry air, because desiccation limits survival and at these temperatures they consume large quantities of water if it is available. However, few individuals can survive for an hour at temperatures above 48°C, and then only at low relative humidities in which they can cool themselves more readily by evaporation. In contrast, at an outside temperature of about

50°C, colonies can maintain their brood area at temperatures of about 35°C indefinitely, and for shorter periods at temperatures as great as 70°C, provided they have access to water.

When the outside temperature approaches the brood area temperature the bees compensate in one or more ways (Fig. 2–5). First, with increase in temperature the bees move further apart in the combs and some leave the nest and cluster outside. With additional increase in environmental temperature bees at the nest entrance face in toward the colony and by fanning their wings draw a current of air out of the nest. Their regulatory activities are reinforced by other bees fanning just inside the entrance and on the combs. When two entrances are available the fanning will be regulated so that air is drawn into one entrance through the combs and out through the other. When there is only one entrance the air may be drawn in through one part of it and forced out through the other. Provided the outside air has a lower temperature than that inside the nest the colony will be cooled. The bees that fan are mostly nest bees; the reason why some but not others do so is unknown.

Because the metabolism of bees increases with temperature, the nest contains more carbon dioxide and less oxygen as the colony gets hotter. Oxygen depletion alone does not release a fanning response, but fanning is induced by increase in the carbon dioxide content of the nest as well as by its increased temperature. Large colonies control their atmospheric carbon dioxide content more precisely than small ones, but it is usually kept at less than 1%; an increase above 3% results in a pronounced increase in fanning (Fig. 2–6).

Bees also cool their colony by evaporating water or dilute nectar. This they accomplish by spreading minute drops of water in the cells, and by regurgitating small drops of water beneath their tongues which are then unfolded, so drawing the water out as a thin film, exposing a relatively large area for evaporation. Water is not stored in the nest but is collected quickly when required (page 37). Bees that evaporate water receive it direct from foragers and carry it to the part of the colony where it is needed.

The brood area of a colony is usually kept at about 40% relative humidity. In the production of honey, bees concentrate nectar by regurgitating it and exposing it beneath their tongues in the same way as when cooling a nest, and when much nectar is being processed in this way the relative humidity becomes excessive. This is again rectified by ventilation fanning and even when the temperature of the air drawn into the nest is greater than that already present, ventilation fanning will continue while the relative humidity inside the nest is too great.

Presumably the bees that are fanning continue to do so only when the air they are replacing is warmer and has a greater carbon dioxide content, or a greater relative humidity, than that outside.

At high environmental temperatures neither ventilation fanning nor

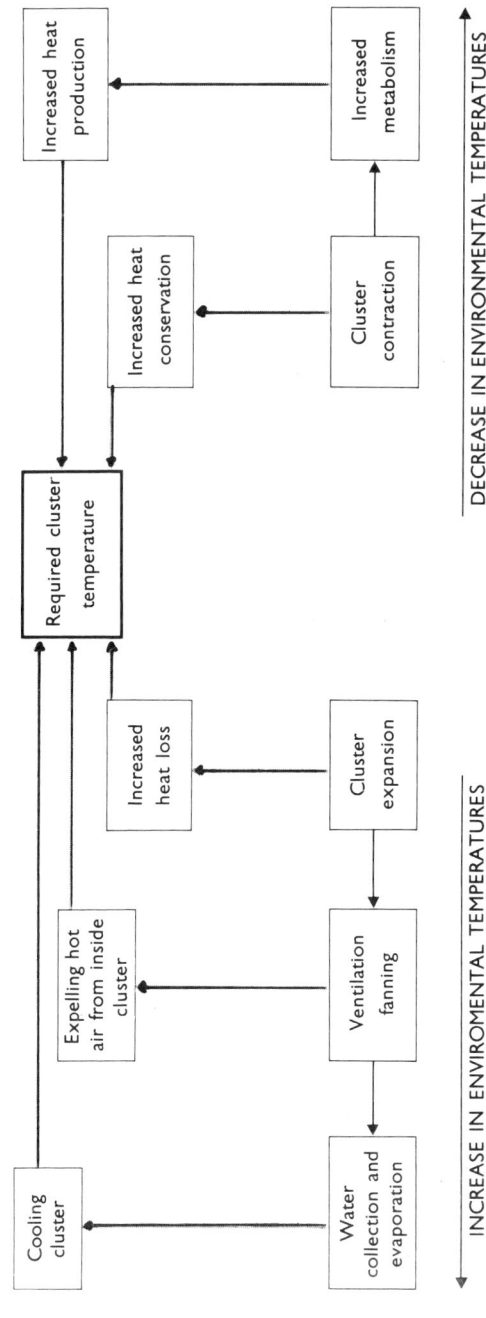

Fig. 2-5 Compensatory mechanisms following a change in environmental temperature.

water evaporation would be adequate on its own. Ventilation fanning without cooling by evaporation would aggravate the situation at outside temperatures above 35%; cooling by evaporation without ventilation would soon saturate the nest atmosphere and cease to be effective.

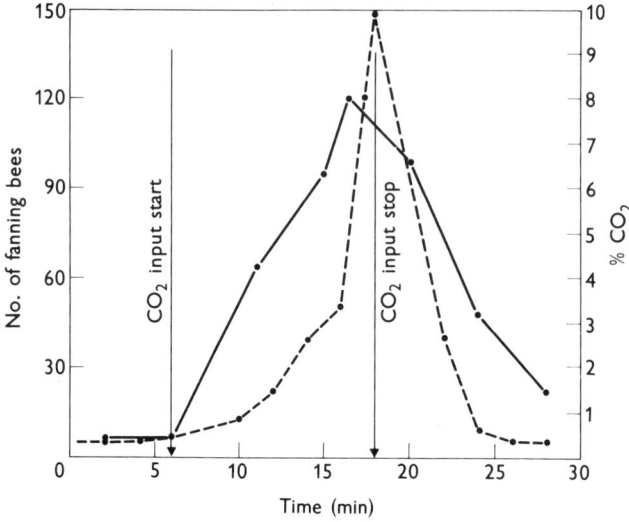

Fig. 2–6 The effect of artificially increasing the carbon dioxide content of a nest atmosphere on the amount of fanning that occurred. (From Seeley, T. D., 1974, *J. Insect Phys.*, **20**, 2301–5.)

2.3.2 Response to low temperature

In conditions under which it cannot collect forage the honeybee colony ceases to rear brood and survives on its accumulated stores of food. In temperate climates this often coincides with low environmental temperatures.

With the onset of cold weather the bees of the colony form a compact cluster which consists of a closely packed mass of bees with sluggish and partially chilled ones on the periphery and warm and active ones inside. Even when bees are kept in small groups of 50 to 200, an increased proportion cluster together as the environmental temperature diminishes from below 20°C and all are clustered at 10°C.

Individual bees have little ability to compensate for increased cold. They are immobilized at about 10°C, and die after 2–3 days at 0–10°C, after only three hours at −3°C and after one hour or less at −4°C, depending to some extent on the temperature at which they have previously been kept. However, the temperature in the centre of a winter cluster is usually between 20 and 30°C, and more often nearer to 30°C.

There are two ways by which bees in a winter cluster compensate for a decrease in environmental temperature; by reduction of heat loss and by increase in heat production (Fig. 2–5). Heat loss can be diminished by contraction of the cluster which decreases its cooling surface, and increases the density of the packing of the bees (in a compact cluster there are 3.3 bees per cm^2), and the winter cluster contracts and expands with decrease and increase in environmental temperature (Fig. 2–7). Decreasing the cluster surface area also results in more heat passing out through each bee at the surface and keeps the cluster from getting too cold.

However, heat loss is complicated by the inclusion of parts of combs within the cluster and these act as cooling fins; so heat loss is not directly proportional to cluster size. The contents of the combs determines their thermal conductivity, empty combs having a much lower conductivity than those filled with honey. The actual heat loss also varies with the structure of the hive or nest and its ventilation.

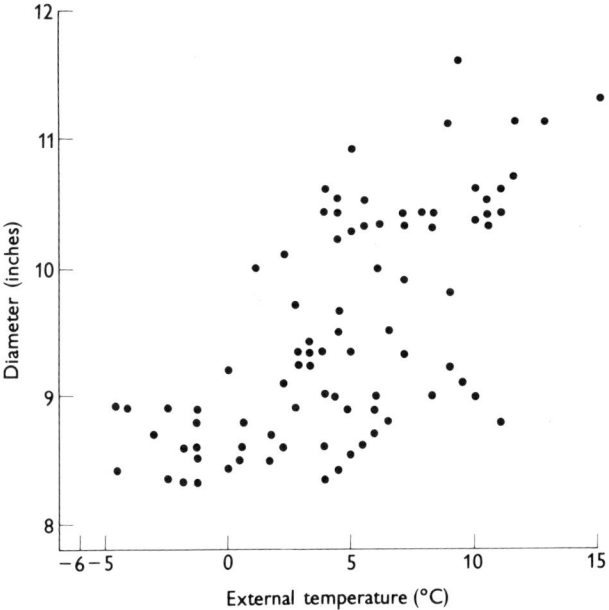

Fig. 2–7 The diameter of a winter cluster at various environmental temperatures. (From Wedmore, E. B., 1953, *J. of Econ. Ent.*, **48**, 723–6 (No. 6).)

The temperature of a winter cluster diminishes from its centre to its edge. The edge of the cluster is at a minimum of 9–10°C. Although bees at the edge of a cluster become acclimatized to some extent to the lower temperature there, if this falls below 9°C they enter a chill coma, fall from the cluster surface and soon die when they are exposed to lower temperatures on the floor of the nest. Differences in the proportions of bees, and their densities at the periphery and the centre of the cluster must influence the temperature gradient between the inside and outside of the cluster, and help to keep the periphery above 9°C, while preventing the centre from becoming too hot or too cold.

Cluster contraction probably reaches its limit at about 5°C, but a cluster of bees can also react to cold weather and adjust the temperature gradient from the inside to the periphery of the cluster by generating more heat.

When only small groups of 25 to 200 bees are exposed to increased cold they increase their rate of metabolism and the amount of food they consume (Fig. 2-8) and are able to keep their temperature higher than the environment (Fig. 2-9). The temperature of the group and its survival rate increases with the group size, but even the small groups are able to survive low temperatures that would quickly kill individual bees. This increased

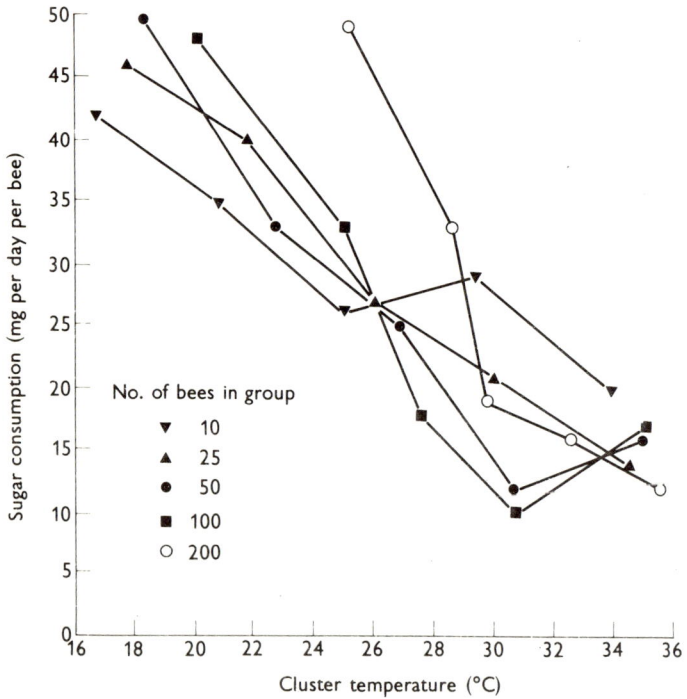

Fig. 2-8 Food consumption of groups of different numbers of bees at different temperatures. (From Simpson, J., 1961, *Science*, **133**, 1327–33, after Free, J. B. and Spencer-Booth, Yvette, 1958, *J. exp. Biol.*, **35**, 930–7. Copyright 1961 by the American Association for the Advancement of Science.)

heat production is achieved by microvibration of the thoracic flight muscles and does not necessarily involve increased visible movement.

The total heat generated by the many thousands of bees in a winter cluster enable it to survive temperatures as low as −40°C. A bee in a winter cluster is at its lowest metabolic rate, as measured by carbon dioxide production (117 μg/bee/h), at +10°C (Fig. 2–10). As the temperature increases above 10°C the increased metabolism reflects increased colony activity at higher temperatures, such as occur in summer, and is not part of the temperature regulating mechanism, but the increase in carbon dioxide production below +10°C reflects the greater metabolism and heat production in response to increased cold. Hence the heat generation by the cluster resembles in some ways the temperature control of homeothermic animals.

Bees at the periphery of a cluster would be the first to perceive a

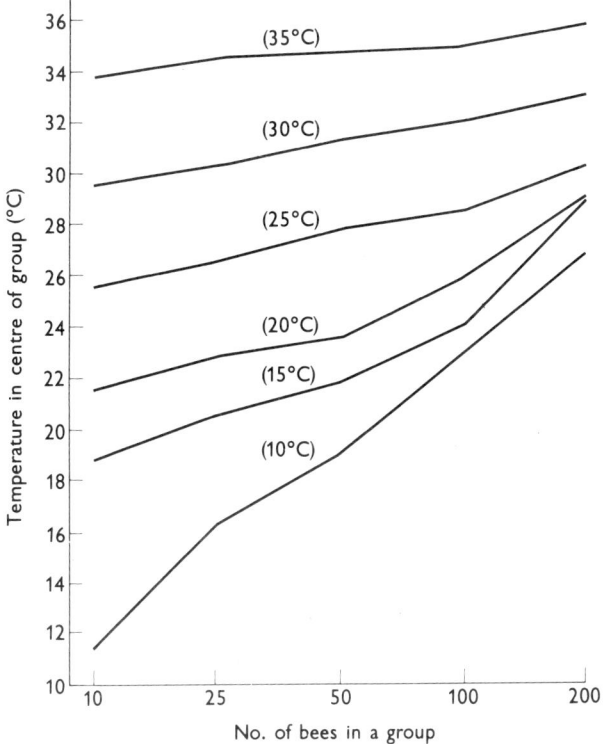

Fig. 2–9 The temperatures which groups of small numbers of bees were able to maintain when exposed to various environmental temperatures (given in brackets). (After Free, J. B. and Spencer-Booth, Yvette, 1958. *J. exp. Biol.*, 35, 930–7.)

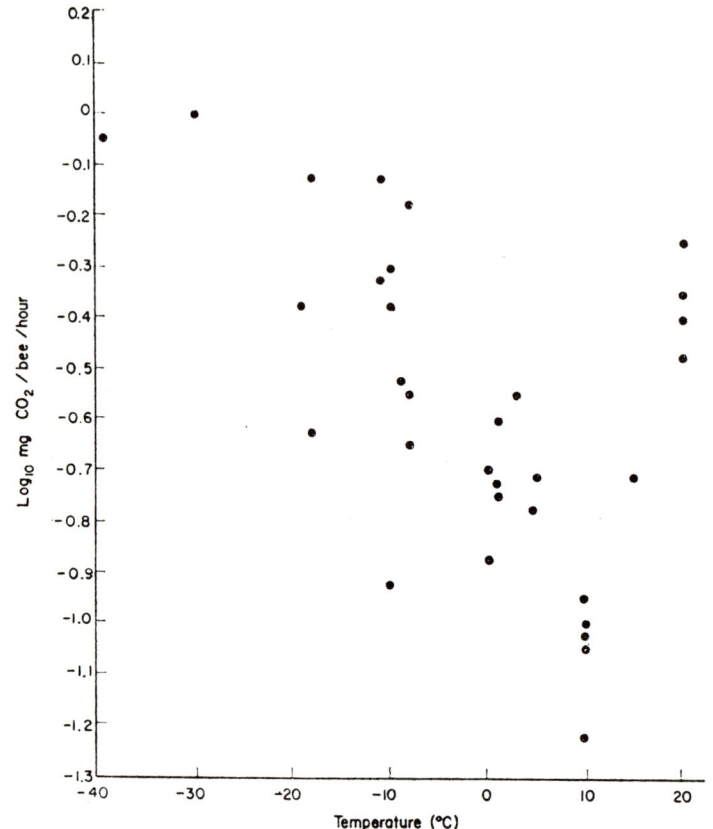

Fig. 2–10 The carbon dioxide output of three honeybee colonies when kept at various environmental temperatures. (After Free, J. B. and Simpson, J., 1963, *Ent. exp. & appl.*, **6**, 234–8.)

lowering of temperature and therefore are probably responsible for initiating regulation by the colony. They may communicate the changed conditions to bees in the centre which then metabolize faster, or themselves move into the colony centre and do so. Attempts made by the peripheral bees to reach the cluster centre when the temperature falls may by itself contribute to cluster contraction.

Because of the smaller ratio of surface area to volume, larger colonies conserve heat more efficiently than smaller ones, and in order to survive cold periods small colonies need to produce more metabolic heat and consume more food per bee than those of large colonies (Fig. 2–11). Large colonies are also more efficient at maintaining the temperatures in their brood areas, early in the year.

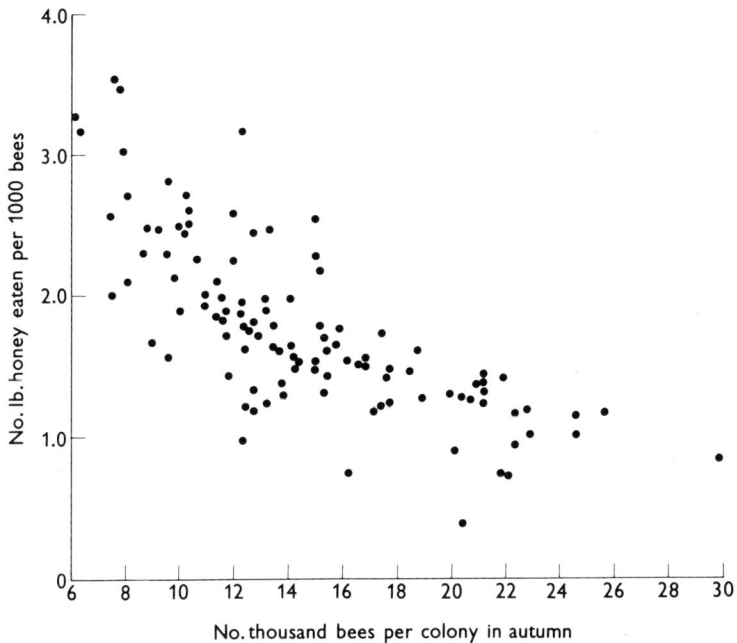

Fig. 2-11 The relationship between the size of colonies in autumn and their food consumption. (From Free, J. B. and Racey, P. A., 1968, *Ent. exp. & appl.*, **11**, 241-9.)

Most work on temperature regulation has been done with *Apis mellifera*. Limited work with *Apis cerana* indicates that although it also responds to low temperature by increased food consumption, indicating increased metabolism and increased heat production, it is less efficient at doing so at low temperatures, and the individual *Apis cerana* bees are more likely to succumb to cold. However, the two species respond similarly to high temperatures. Hence although *Apis cerana* is less adapted to temperate climates than *Apis mellifera*, it does not appear to have any special corresponding adaptations to the tropics.

2.4 Co-ordination of activities and communication within the nest

Much work has been done in the last two decades to attempt to discover how bees communicate with each other inside the nest and co-ordinate their activities. Within the darkness or semi-darkness of the nest or hive, visual systems can be of little or no importance, and the known senses by which bees could recognize and signal to each other are auditory, tactile or chemical. Substrate sound may be used as a source of communication in a few specific circumstances (pages 44, 54 and 56) but bees do not perceive airborne sound. The thousands of individuals of a honeybee colony are constantly touching each other and frequently make antennal contact but no definite form of tactile language has been discovered so it seems unlikely that antennal contact has evolved into a highly developed code system. Communication by chemicals whether perceived as taste or smell, is of prime importance. Worker bees are particularly adept at perceiving the individual scents in a mixture and at discriminating between mixtures containing different proportions of the same scents. One way chemical communication can occur is by transfer of food.

2.4.1 Transfer of food

In a honeybee colony food is passed directly from one worker bee to another, as well as from workers to drones and the queen, and acts as an important integrating mechanism. The food given is water, nectar or honey regurgitated from the honeystomach; it may also, sometimes consist of, or contain, glandular secretions.

The transfer of food between two bees arises as a result of one of them either begging food from, or offering food to, the other (Fig. 2–12). A bee that is begging for food attempts to thrust its proboscis between the mandibles of another. A bee that is offering food opens its mandibles and moves its still-folded proboscis slightly downwards and forwards from its position of rest; a drop of regurgitated food can often be seen between the

Fig. 2–12 Food transfer between two worker bees. The bee on the left with extended tongue is receiving food from the bee on the right.

mandibles and in the proximal part of the proboscis. Queens and drones as well as workers beg for food, but usually only workers offer it. During feeding, the antennae of both giver and receiver of food are in constant motion and are continually coming into contact.

Both begging and offering behaviour are innate reactions and improve with age independently of conditioning. They can both be released by an excised head that is mounted on a pin at the 'normal' height and position. However, only a few of a number of possible features act as releasers. Thus, the odour of a head is a most important stimulus, and bees sometimes even beg from 'model' heads consisting of small balls of cotton wool which have been rubbed against bees' heads and have presumably acquired something of their odour. In contrast, the colour and shape of the heads is of little importance and hungry bees beg from the lowest part of a head irrespective of its orientation.

The antennae are also a very important contact stimulus in releasing food transference and in helping bees to orientate their mouth parts to one another. It is possible to simulate their effect by inserting two small pieces of wire of approximately the same length and diameter as real antennae, into heads from which the antennae have been removed.

A worker bee obtains all its food directly from other bees for the first two days of its life, and does not help itself from the colony's food storage cells until it is about three days old. Although even very young bees may give food, in general until bees are about two weeks old they generally receive food more often than they give it although thereafter the opposite tends to be true. Furthermore, in general, individuals receive food from bees that are older than those to which they give it, and as workers grow older the average ages of bees that they feed, and are fed by, also increases. As a consequence there is a tendency for food to pass rapidly and widely through a colony from older bees which are foragers to bees that are feeding brood, or producing wax, or ripening the nectar to produce honey. In one experiment foragers were allowed to collect a small quantity (20 cm^3) of sugar syrup containing radioactive phosphorus and it was found that within 24 h it had become disseminated among 55% of the bees of their colony.

Hence, changes in both the quality and quantity of incoming nectar supplies are rapidly appreciated. As these changes can affect many activities including egg-laying, brood rearing, ripening and storing of honey, wax secretion and comb building, food transfer is an important means of communication.

Furthermore, the food being circulated also determines: the threshold concentration of nectar acceptable for foragers which varies greatly at different times of the year (page 41); the need for nectar (page 39), and the need for water (page 37). The small amount of nectar given by a successful forager to potential foragers within the nest informs them of both the scent and taste of the forage they are to seek (page 42).

2.4.2 Pheromones

The prime means of chemical communication within the nest is by pheromones. These are chemical substances, produced and discharged externally by an individual, that elicit specific behavioural or physiological responses in another individual of the same species. Thus they enable the members of a honeybee colony to communicate by a code of chemical stimuli. The first honeybee pheromone to be discovered is one which is released in the field or at the nest entrance by worker honeybees and attracts other honeybees in the vicinity (Fig. 2–13). Pheromones released by a stinging worker attract other guard bees to the alien target. Within the nest the pheromones produced by the brood both stimulate workers to forage and inhibit the development of the workers' ovaries.

Fig. 2–13 A forager that has returned to its nest entrance is exposing its Nasanov gland and fanning with its wings. This helps disorientated bees in the vicinity to find their way home.

However, our knowledge of honeybee pheromones is at best fragmentary because the task of identifying and characterizing them is proving far from easy. This is partly because in different circumstances the same pheromone may have different meanings. Thus there are 32 or more pheromones produced in the head of a queen (relatively few of which have been identified chemically) giving innumerable possible combinations, in some of which the pheromones may act synergistically. The concentration of pheromone produced, the duration of its

§ 2.4   CO-ORDINATION OF ACTIVITIES AND COMMUNICATION   29

production, and its persistence may all vary, and the same pheromone may have different effects in different contexts (page 66). Furthermore, although long chain paraffins in the cuticular wax of honeybees tend to act as fixitives for more volatile pheromones, all or part of the pheromone complex is often highly volatile and does not lend itself readily to current techniques of analysis.

Consequently it is not surprising that some results of pheromone studies are difficult to interpret, and that frequently apparently conflicting data are obtained. These difficulties are sometimes reinforced by differences, probably not always appreciated, in the conditions of the bioassay, in the strain of bee concerned, and in the responses given by physiologically different bees.

Hence, even though the complexity and importance of pheromones in the social organization of the honeybee colony is fully appreciated, few have been characterized, and none of the systems that operate within the nest have been completely simulated by synthetic materials.

There are three ways by which pheromones could be transferred between bees: in the air, by physical contact and in the food, but often the mechanism of transfer is not known with certainty.

The enclosed interior of the type of nest usually occupied by honeybees of the species *Apis mellifera* and *Apis cerana* (e.g. dark crevices, caves, hollow trees) would appear to facilitate information transfer by airborne volatile pheromones. An almost constant temperature and absence of wind currents would enhance the stability of pheromone production and dissemination, whereas regulated nest ventilation by fanning bees could rapidly disperse or dispel pheromones when necessary.

Although no form of antennal 'language' has been discovered, the antennae contain numerous sensilla cells, a single one of which may be sensitive to a single molecule of pheromone, so it is quite feasible for the antennae to both perceive and transfer pheromones.

As well as being a means of communication itself, the food has been suggested as a medium in which various pheromones are circulated through the colony. However, there is some doubt as to whether pheromones could be disseminated quickly enough by this method, or indeed whether the bee's ability to perceive the pheromones would be masked by the sugar in the food.

3 Colony Defence

3.1 Introduction

Because the honeybee's nest contains stores of honey and pollen and often an abundance of brood, it attracts the attention of many potential robbers, including man. The aggressive behaviour that defending bees exhibit to such intruding aliens is a fundamental necessity if their colony is to survive.

3.2 Defensive mechanisms

A bee's sting is barbed, so that when it is used against a bird or mammal it becomes embedded in the soft flesh. When the bee attempts to withdraw it the sting and the seventh abdominal segment are broken off and left *in situ*. The last nerve ganglion and the muscles that operate the poison sac are left with the sting, so it continues to inject venom (comprised mostly of a complex mixture of peptides) into the victim's body. The bee that has stung soon dies, but the sacrifice of a few individuals may deter a large intruder that could destroy their entire colony.

Effective defence is dependent upon rapid recognition of the enemy. The prime means of recognition is by odour, but other factors may also be involved in stimulating aggressive behaviour. They have been studied by using a technique dependent on sting autotomy. When cotton or leather balls, 2-3 cm diameter, are suspended or jerked in front of a nest entrance, many of the bees that attack them will leave their stings behind. The ferocity of the attack may be determined by counting the stings. Using this technique it has been shown that aggressiveness is readily released by dark colours, mammal odour including that of human sweat, rough texture and rapid jerking movements.

Once a ball has received one sting it is likely to receive further stings, so a sting left behind in an enemy has the effect of 'marking' the target area and facilitating further defensive onslaughts. This is not due to any odour of the sting venom itself but to the release of a highly volatile pheromone, isopentyl acetate, $(CH_3)_2CHCH_2CH_2OCOCH_3$, which is produced by cells lining the sting pouch (Fig. 1-3). When a bee that has stung literally tears itself away from its victim the exposed isopentylacetate rapidly evaporates attracting other workers to the source.

The same pheromone is also often discharged without stinging and functions as a chemical alarm system. The alerted worker elevates its abdomen, opens its sting chamber, protrudes its sting and in so doing erects and exposes the membrane in which the pheromone is stored. By fanning its wings the bee helps disperse the pheromone. This behaviour alerts and attracts other bees at the nest and stimulates them to investigate and if necessary attack an enemy in the vicinity. The release of isopentyl acetate at the nest entrance also has the complementary effect of reducing the numbers of departing foragers, so the defensive force of the colony is increased.

Bees stinging an enemy often grip it with their mandibles and the mandibular glands of bees that are guards or foragers also produce another pheromone, 2-heptanone $CH_3(CH_2)_4CO\ CH_3$, that also appears to have an alarm or alerting function. However, isopentyl acetate is many times more powerful; 2-heptanone requires concentrations 20 to 70 times greater than isopentyl acetate to evoke similar alarm reactions from bees at the nest entrance. All four *Apis* species produce isopentyl acetate, but only *Apis mellifera* also produces 2-heptanone.

In common with other chemical alarm systems these pheromones have a rapid fading response and so prevent the colony from being in an unnecessarily prolonged state of turmoil; unless continued danger provides a positive feed back, the state of alertness will soon return to normal.

3.3 Aggressiveness

Colonies of different genetic constitution may differ greatly in their aggressiveness. The aggressive characteristics of a strain of African bee (*Apis mellifera adonsonii*) that was accidently released in Brazil in 1956 is now spreading through the honeybees in South America. Differences in temperament between an Italian and an African colony are shown in the following typical test:

	Italian colony	African colony
No. stings in small leather ball suspended before nest entrance	26	64
Time before first sting occurred	19 s	3 s
Time taken to become fierce	23 s	7 s
Distance bees followed observer after they became very fierce	23 m	170 m
Time taken to become peaceful	149 s	1801 s

Increased aggressiveness tends to be correlated both with increase in the amount of isopentyl acetate the bees produce and a lower threshold of response to it.

It has long been known by beekeepers that blowing smoke at a honeybee colony lessens its aggressive tendencies. The smoke causes about half the bees to engorge themselves with honey from the comb, and those that do so are less likely to sting than those that do not. Bees engaged in feeding brood or building comb have more food in their honeystomachs than those engaged in other activities both before and after smoking, so they would probably be less likely to leave the combs and attack an intruder. However, because many bees of all ages do not engorge when their colonies are smoked it seems that other effects of smoke are important to the beekeeper; perhaps smoke inhibits aggressiveness by deterring bees from leaving their combs, by distracting their attention from the intruder, by masking the intruder's alien scent, or by masking the alarm pheromones produced and so impeding the spread of alarm.

3.4 Guard bees

After bees have completed nest duty and before they begin to forage some become guards. The numbers that do so increase with the numbers of potential intruders, which is greater at some times than others. This is particularly true of those insect intruders whose abundance is seasonally controlled, and when forage is scarce and their colony is in danger of being robbed, a large proportion of the bees, including out-of-work foragers undertake guard duty.

Guard bees frequently assume a typical 'threat posture' with their front legs off the ground, antennae held forwards, and their mandibles and wings open, ready to rush toward any intruder (Fig. 3–1). Each guard

Fig. 3–1 An alert guard bee.

tends to patrol a particular part of the nest entrance, sometimes for a period of an hour or more, but may disappear within the nest or go foraging between spells of guard duty. There is great variation in individual dedication to guarding the colony; 'zealous' guards may remain on duty for up to 4 days, while others remain inside the nest entrance and soon become foragers. The duration of guard duty probably increases with the frequency of alien attack.

The tendency for individuals to become guards is probably linked with various physiological factors including venom production and ovary growth. Aggressiveness in the worker caste of social insects is usually associated with ovary development and bees that are guards have better developed ovaries than normal.

When intruding insects of other species (e.g. a wasp or bumblebee) attempt to enter their nest the guard bees rapidly pounce on them and attempt to thrust their stings between the intruders' intersegmental membranes; several guards often attack the same intruder. Unless the intruder manages to break away, either it or the guard is usually killed. Stinging is not always the most effective defence; honeybees have been seen to repel invading ants by turning directly in front of them so as to face the same direction as the advancing ants, and then to kick backwards with their rear legs and vigorously fan air backwards with their wings to dislodge the ants.

3.5 Recognition of intruders

The most serious threats to a honeybee colony often come from the bees of other colonies nearby which, during periods of dearth, attempt to steal its honey stores. To defend their colony guard bees must be able to distinguish workers of their own and other colonies. This they are able to do partly by the behaviour of the bee they are examining and partly by its odour.

All the adult workers in a colony share the same colony odour which is different from that of any other colony. It appears that this odour is not inherited but is acquired from the environment. The cuticular waxes of the bees' bodies absorb the odours inside the nest. The odour of the stored food is probably the main one concerned, and as the floral sources of the food a colony collects are continually changing, so also is the odour common to the bees of the colony.

Guards frequently intercept members of their own colony at the nest entrance. They often try to examine the abdomen of the bee they have intercepted and their behaviour suggests that they need to approach a suspect very closely and touch it with their antenna, before they are certain of its identity. When the bee being examined has the same identifying odour as the guard itself, it seldom hesitates for more than a second or so, and if it is a returning forager, it continues into the nest

(Fig. 3–2). A guard seldom tries to examine a member of its own colony for more than 2 to 3 seconds.

In modern apiaries, with regular rows of hives, bees frequently stray by mistake into hives other than their own. When the bee that has inadvertently strayed is returning from a successful foraging expedition it walks into the hive without hesitation and when intercepted by guards it rarely stops and submits to examination. Guard bees often follow it, examining its abdomen, but do not molest it. The guard bees spend much more time examining these 'dominant' intruders than foragers of their own colony, and since the behaviour of the two types of forager is the same, recognize them by their strange odours.

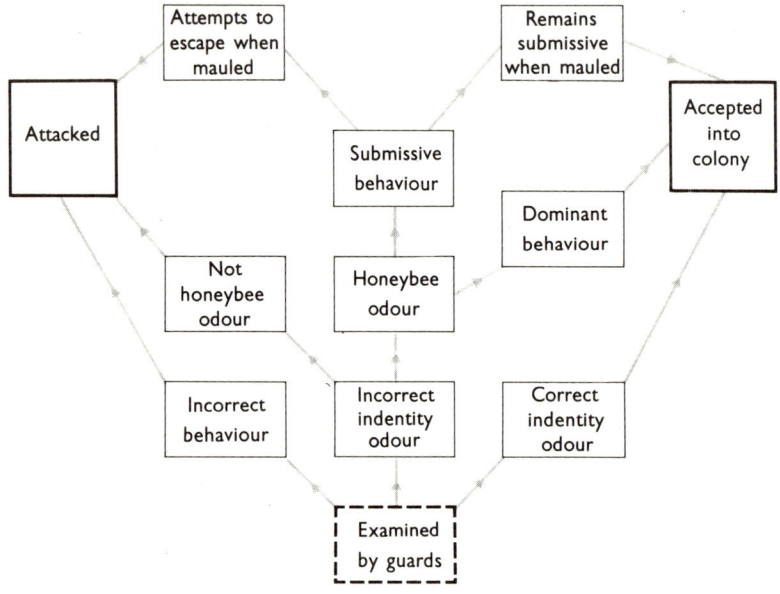

Fig. 3–2 Fate of intruders to honeybee colonies.

In contrast, when bees that have inadvertently strayed to a strange hive during their orientation flights and have not been foraging, are intercepted by guards they stop moving toward the hive entrance and adopt a typical submissive attitude with the tips of their abdomens tucked in. Often, several guards simultaneously examine the same intruder and frequently some of them proceed to maul it, pulling at its legs, wings and head, and attempting to drag it away from the hive entrance. Sometimes, when a submissive intruder is being mauled, its legs are quickly and simultaneously jerked from the ground causing it to enter an entirely motionless and passive state, in which it allows itself to be carried by the guards.

§ 3.5   RECOGNITION OF INTRUDERS

When a guard approaches the head of a submissive intruder, the intruder offers it a drop of regurgitated food. This offer of food is usually ignored, but even when it is accepted other guards continue to maul the intruder while it is actually giving food, and the guard that accepts food often mauls the intruder afterwards. Although the function of this behaviour is obscure it is interesting because perhaps the transfer of food between worker honeybees has evolved from the habit of a submissive bee offering food to a dominant. Observations on bumblebees support this; although there is usually no food transfer between bumblebee workers, when a bumblebee worker is attacked by another it sometimes regurgitates a drop of food.

When offers of food by a submissive intruder have been ignored several times it extends its tongue which it commences to strop with its front pair of legs. This behaviour is similar to the normal tongue cleaning behaviour of bees except the movements are faster, less complete and the process continues for much longer. It, and other examples of self-grooming, have been compared to the activities of vertebrates that can arise in the presence of two conflicting drives, (e.g. to flee and to fight). Probably this behaviour by the submissive bee in some way appeases the aggressive tendencies of the guards; perhaps it is associated with the release of an anti-antagonistic pheromone.

Unless the intruders attempt to break away, which immediately releases the guards' stinging response, the guards do not attempt to kill submissive intruders, and some of them are eventually allowed to enter the hive, and after a few hours are no longer examined or mauled by bees of the recipient colony, presumably because they have now acquired its odour.

Although inadvertent intruders are recognized by their strange odours, bees that attempt to rob colonies of their stores of honey are recognized by their jerky swaying flight, as they move too and fro in front of the hive entrance, attempting to enter unchallenged by the guards.

In one experiment bees were trained to 'rob' honey from an otherwise empty hive and about half of the robber bees' own colony, including the queen, was then transferred to the empty hive. As soon as the transferred bees were released their guards attempted to grab the robber bees, although when they succeeded in so doing, they quickly released them, suggesting the identifying odour of the robbers had inhibited stinging.

It is difficult to see the advantage to the robber bees of their characteristic darting flight; perhaps it may facilitate their escape; because it is initiated by a congestion at the hive entrance, it is conceivable that it acts as a social releaser that alerts other members of their colony that approach the hive.

Directly a guard bee has grabbed a robber from another colony it attempts to sting; the robber retaliates in a similar manner, and fighting continues until one is killed.

Therefore, although a series of stimuli including jerky movements, dark colours and alien odours evoke the attacks of guard bees the correct odours or correct behaviour patterns preserve the lives of members of their own colony, and of inadvertent intruders, and so help the colony to survive.

4 Collection of Forage

4.1 Factors determining type of forage collected

In addition to nectar and pollen foragers collect propolis and water. The type and quantity of forage collected is related to colony needs at the time.

4.1.1 Propolis

Propolis is a resinous exudate from the bark or buds of various trees. Bees use it for filling cracks and small openings in the walls of nests and for reducing larger openings. When a propolis forager returns home it goes to a part of the nest where propolis is needed and waits for a cementing bee to remove the propolis from its corbiculae. Propolis is normally collected in late summer and autumn during the warmest part of the day.

All bees that collect propolis also use it in the nest, the cementing being done later in the day than the foraging; so propolis foragers must have direct awareness of the propolis requirements. However, not all cementing bees forage for propolis although, as they are the older bees engaged in nest tasks, and are probably aware of the supply and demand, they presumably forage when necessary.

4.1.2 Water

Water is not stored in the comb but is collected as needed. It is used to dilute honey stores when producing brood-food, especially in the spring when little nectar is available. Water carriers are particularly numerous after cool or rainy weather during which bees have been unable to collect nectar and have had to use stored honey.

When the inside of the nest becomes too hot, the nest bees cool it by putting droplets of water on the comb and increase evaporation by fanning it with their wings; they also assist cooling by evaporating nectar and water on their tongues (page 18).

The need for water inside the nest is communicated to foragers indirectly through the transfer of food. As more water is used in a colony and the need for it becomes greater, the concentration of food in the honeystomachs of the nest bees increases and they accept loads more eagerly and quickly from foragers that have collected the most dilute nectar or water, whereas concentrated nectar is accepted hesitantly or rejected. This encourages water gatherers to make recruiting dances (Fig. 4–1) and mark the site of the water with Nasonov gland odour (page 46), and nectar gatherers to change to collecting water (Fig. 4–2).

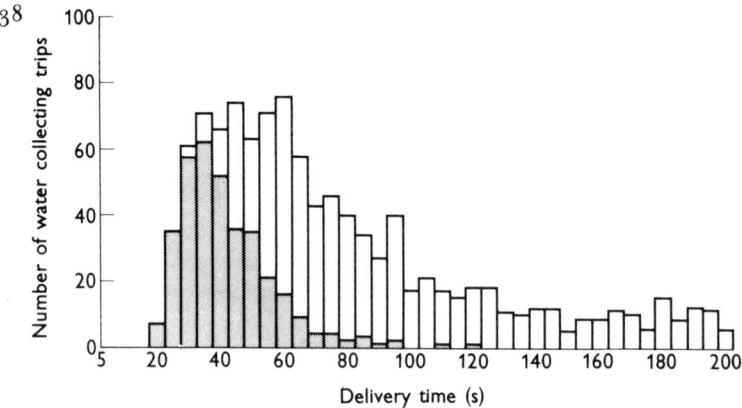

Fig. 4-1 Relationship between the time water collectors take to deliver their loads to nest bees and the number of trips followed by communication dances (tinted columns) and not followed by communication dances (white columns). (After Lindauer, M., 1955, *Bee World*, **36**, 62–72, 81–92, 105–11.)

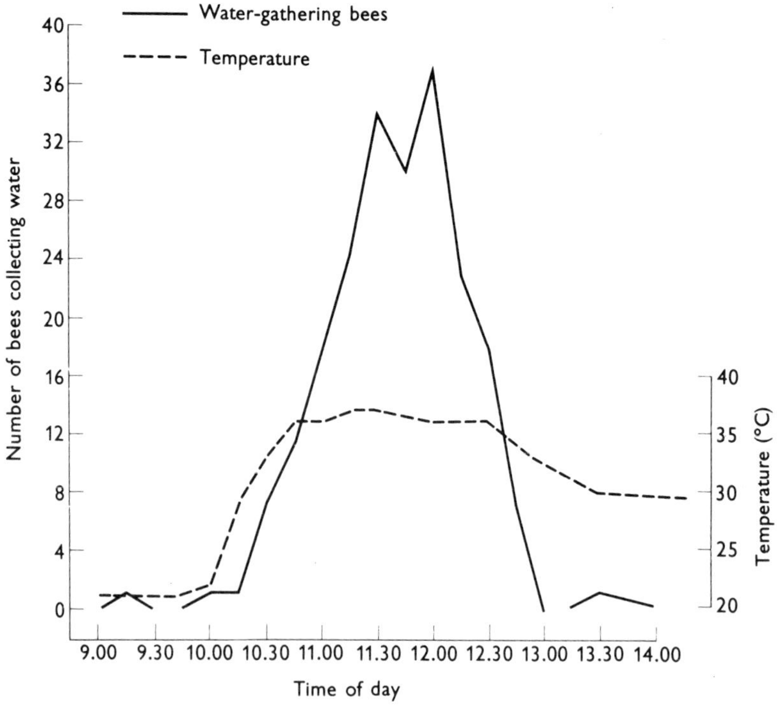

Fig. 4-2 Relationship between the environmental temperature and the number of bees collecting water. (After Lindauer, M., 1955, *Bee World*, **36**, 62–72, 81–92, 105–11.)

When the need for water lessens, foragers with loads of water have difficulty in getting nest bees to accept it, and the eagerness and rapidity with which nest bees accept loads of nectar increases with its concentration. When the delivery time exceeds three minutes, foraging for water practically ceases. Hence, at those times when there is a small demand for water only a few foragers collect it between trips for nectar and pollen. But when water is urgently needed these bees know the location of water and can inform others.

4.1.3 Pollen

The collection of pollen is greatly influenced by the needs of the colony. Although honeybees obtain only pollen from some flowers (e.g. *Papaver* sp.), and nectar but little pollen from others (e.g. *Tilia europoea*, *Ribes nigrum*), they can collect loads of both nectar and pollen from most species. Foragers often collect pollen on some trips, but nectar on others on the same day. The type of forage collected depends partly on its availability, and in some flower species pollen and nectar are most abundant at different times of the day. However, some bees collect nectar only, others pollen only, and others nectar and pollen on the same crop at the same time. Evidently, therefore, individual foragers decide the type of forage they will collect, and it has been shown that they quickly change from collecting nectar to collecting pollen and vice versa as their colony's requirements change.

Provided there are adequate honey stores in the colony, with increase in the amount of brood the proportion of foragers that collect pollen and the amount of pollen collected also increases (Fig. 4-3). In contrast,

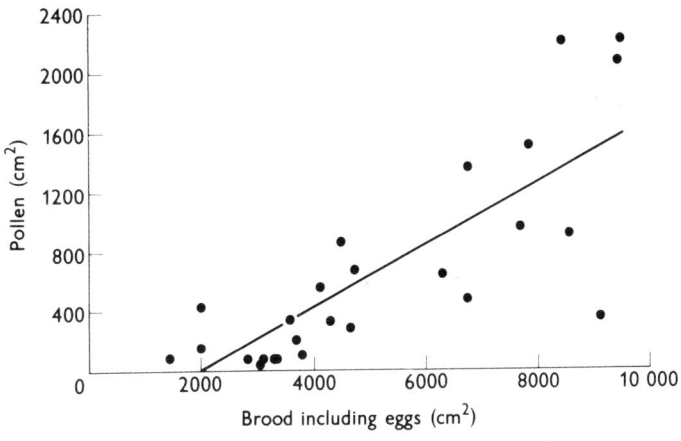

Fig. 4-3 The relationship between the total amount of brood and the amount of stored pollen present in honeybee colonies. (From Free, J. B. and Williams, Ingrid H., 1975, *Anim. Behav.*, **23**, 650–75.)

depriving colonies of brood causes many pollen-gatherers to change to collecting nectar only.

Pollen-gatherers deposit their loads directly into storage cells, and so cannot receive information about pollen requirements from recipient bees as nectar-gatherers do. However, the eagerness with which the pollen loads of a returned forager are examined by nest bees may influence its subsequent foraging behaviour and encourage it to recruit further pollen-gatherers. Pollen is put into cells next to the batches of brood as well as in combs adjacent to the brood area so it is possible that they could obtain direct information.

Although brood of all stages stimulates pollen collection the larval stage is particularly effective.

The smell of the brood alone and contact with bees tending the brood are each partly responsible for foragers collecting pollen, but individual foragers must have access to the brood if they are to receive maximum stimulation to collect pollen. Evidently the larvae produce a pheromone that stimulates pollen collection.

The amount of pollen collected is also influenced by the pollen stores present, and giving pollen to a colony diminishes pollen collection and increases nectar collection. Perhaps foragers ascertain the pollen requirements directly by inspecting brood and pollen cells, but this presupposes that they can correlate requirements with amounts of stores. Probably when a brood feeding bee has difficulty in finding pollen it prepares cells to receive pollen loads so that the number of cells increases with increase in pollen requirements. Perhaps the amount of pollen collected depends on the frequency with which foragers find empty pollen storage cells and thus on the rapidity with which they can deposit their pollen loads.

Irrespective of the presence of the brood the queen also induces pollen collection. Experiments have demonstrated that it is possible to simulate the function of the queen to some extent by providing small queenless colonies with the queen pheromone, 9-oxo-*trans*-2-decenoic acid (see page 50).

4.1.4 Nectar

Surprisingly, factors that encourage nectar collection have been little studied. It is not known whether the amount of nectar collected is related to the amount of honey stored, although nectar collection extends far beyond the immediate needs of the colony.

Although feeding sugar syrup to a colony increases pollen collection, this does not seem to be because the colony's need for carbohydrate is satisfied, but rather because the nest bees that normally receive nectar loads are collecting the syrup, and nectar-gatherers have difficulty in passing on their nectar and so change to pollen collection.

Nectar is probably collected in the absence of a special need for pollen, propolis or water. The presence of brood and the queen of a colony stimulate foraging in general, including nectar collection.

4.2 Attractiveness of forage

The supply of forage fluctuates with the time of year and the flowering of various crops. When crops are in flower the amount of forage available varies with temperature, weather and day length. These factors must govern the number of wild colonies which can survive unaided in an area. The duration of time for which forage is available can be as important as its total abundance.

The attractiveness of a particular crop in flower depends upon many factors including the quality and quantity of pollen produced per flower, the concentration and quantity of nectar produced per flower, the concentration and abundance of the flowers, the number of competing insects, the attractiveness of competing crops, the distance of the crop from the colony, the requirements of the colony, and the colony's innate floral preference.

All of these factors are subject to variation so the attractiveness of a crop to honeybees may differ in different circumstances. The foraging of honeybees themselves on a crop will eventually diminish its attractiveness (Fig. 4-4).

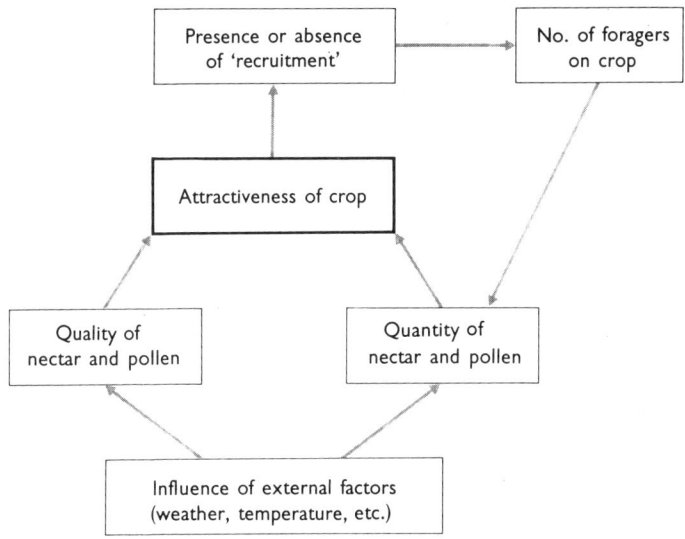

Fig. 4-4 Factors determining the attractiveness of a crop to honeybee foragers.

4.3 Dance language

Foragers are able to inform other members of their colony of the location of an attractive supply of forage, and this enables them to exploit it rapidly, although the threshold at which a crop is attractive enough to encourage recruitment also varies considerably.

When the forage is located within 25 metres of the colony, on its return home, the successful forager performs a 'round dance' in which it describes a series of circles on the comb surface, alternating between a clockwise and an anticlockwise direction every one or two circles (Fig. 4–5). The dance may go through only one or two reversals, or as many as twenty.

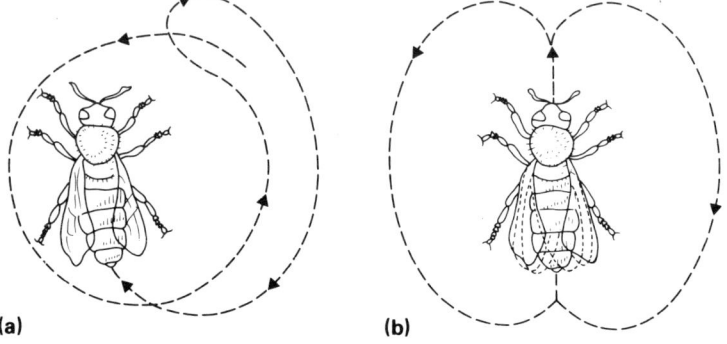

(a) (b)

Fig. 4–5 Honeybee dances. (a) Round dance. (b) Tail-wagging dance. (From FRISCH, K. VON 1950, *Bees: Their Vision, Chemical Senses, and Language*, New York, Cornell University Press, and London, Jonathan Cape.)

Some of the nearby bees, that are stimulated by the dancer, touch her with their antennae and attempt to follow her (Fig. 4–5). The dancer, at intervals interrupts her dance to offer these potential recruits a drop of the nectar she has collected. The potential recruits learn the odour of the forage they are to seek from the odour of the nectar they are given, and from the odour of the flowers adhering to the body of the dancing bee. They pay particular attention to any pollen loads. Recruited foragers usually leave their nest within a minute or so and seek forage of the correct odour in its vicinity. Recruitment increases with the liveliness and vigour of the dance and with its duration.

When the forage is located 100 metres or more away from its nest a successful forager performs a 'tail wagging' dance (Fig. 4–5). It moves a short distance in a straight line or 'run', makes a semi-circle back to the beginning of the run, moves forward again to the top of the run, makes another semi-circle back to the beginning of the run, but in the opposite direction, and then repeats the process. This dance, in contrast with the general 'alerting' nature of the round dance, describes the direction and distance of the food source (Fig. 4–6).

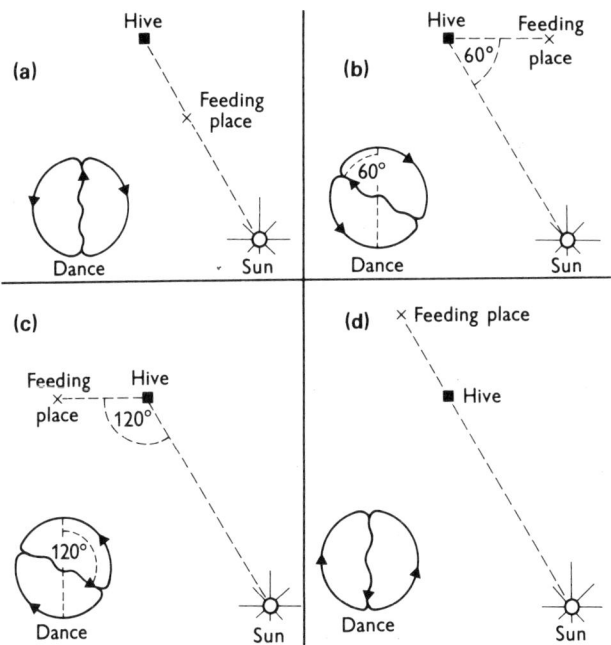

Fig. 4–6 Relationship between the angle of the straight part of the tail-wagging dance on the vertical comb and the angle between the feeding place, sun and hive. (From FRISCH, K. VON, 1954, *The Dancing Bees*, London, Methuen.)

The direction is given by the angle the straight run makes with the vertical; it is the same as the angle between the direction of food and the direction of the sun as measured from the nest. The bees are somehow able to transpose the gravitational stimuli in the nest for the visual stimuli in the field and vice versa. Furthermore, with change in position of the sun in the sky during the day, the bees are able to change the angle of their dance. It is hardly surprising that the accuracy of a particular dance increases with its performance.

If the comb on which a bee is dancing is removed from the hive and tilted to the horizontal the bee then orientates its straight run direct to the target food source. This is the sole method of direction indication used by *Apis florea* foragers, which dance on the horizontal top of their single exposed comb. *Apis dorsata* foragers dance on the vertical surface of the comb, but need to be able to see the sun or blue sky to be able to do so. *Apis cerana* like *Apis mellifera* is able to perform 'tail wagging' dances in the darkness of the nest.

During the straight run the dancer rapidly waggles its abdomen, 13 to 15 times per second, (hence the name of the dance) and by vibrating its

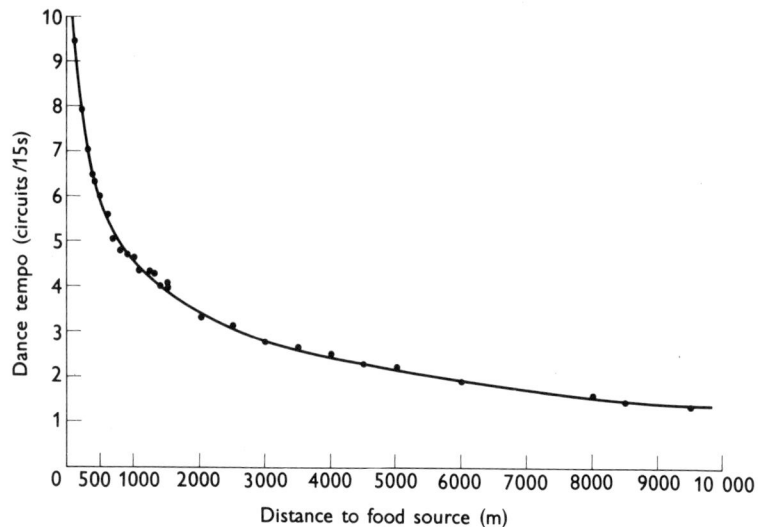

Fig. 4–7 Relationship between the tempo of the tail-wagging dance, as measured by the number of circuits per 15-second periods, and the distance to the source of forage. (From FRISCH, K. VON, 1967, *The Dance Language and Orientation of Bees*, London, Oxford University Press, and Cambridge, Mass., the Belknap Press of Harvard University Press, Copyright © 1967 by the President and Fellows of Harvard College.)

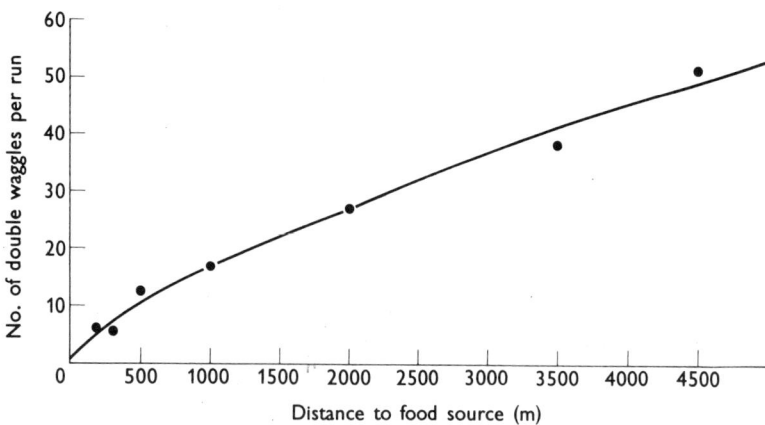

Fig. 4–8 Relationship between the number of waggles per straight run part of the tail-wagging dance and the distance from the food source. (From FRISCH, K. VON, 1967, *The Dance Language and Orientation of Bees*, publisher and copyright as 4–7.)

wings emits a pulsated sound of approximately 200–250 cycles per second. The duration of the straight run, of the dance circuit (Fig. 4–7), and the number of waggles (Fig. 4–8) are positively correlated with the distance of the food source from the nest. There is less certainty that the duration of sound production during the straight run and the number of sound pulses during the straight run, are also correlated with distance. It appears that the dancing bee evaluates the distance to the target area from the energy it spent on the *outward* flight. The further the forage from the nest, the further from the nest entrance the forager is likely to dance.

As in the round dance, the performer of a 'tail wagging' dance gives food at intervals to potential recruits that are following its manœuvres. The exact nature of the clues and stimuli perceived and reacted upon by the potential recruits is still not fully understood, but the success of a recruit in finding the food source increases with the number of dances it has followed before leaving the nest.

The 'round' and 'tail wagging' dances are not sharply demarcated, but when the distance of the food source is between about 25 and 100 metres from the nest, dances (usually 'sickle' dances) that are transitional between 'round' and 'tail wagging' are performed (Fig. 4–9).

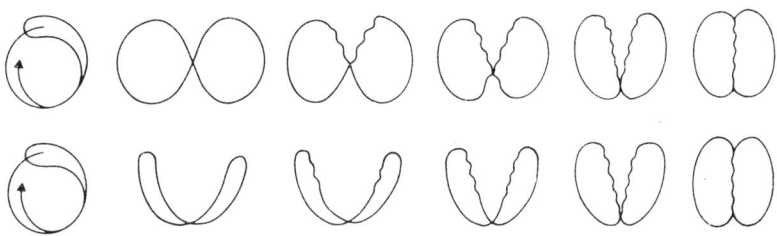

Fig. 4–9 Diagrammatic transitions from round dance to tail-wagging dance. (After FRISCH, K. VON, 1967, *The Dance Language and Orientation of Bees*, publisher and copyright as 4–7.)

Recent carefully controlled experiments have confirmed earlier findings on these communicative functions of the waggle dance. It has even been possible to send recruits to a target area by using a 'dummy' bee that was made to dance on the comb at different angles to the vertical and at different frequencies.

Under natural conditions bees recruited to a source of forage do not follow the dance direction very precisely (Figs. 4–10 and 4–11), but it is not necessary nor desirable that they should do so. A natural food crop, whose location is worth communicating, is likely to be distributed over a considerable area, and if the arrival points of the recruits are also widely distributed, a colony can exploit it more efficiently than if all its foragers concentrated on a small area.

However, most naturally occurring water sites are more discrete than those of nectar or pollen and have less pronounced odours. When a

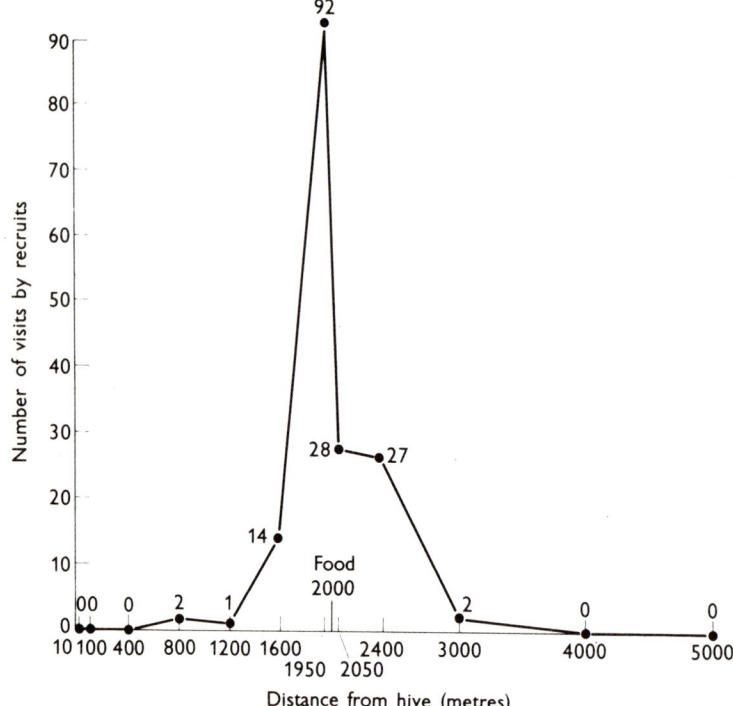

Fig. 4–10 Communication of distance. Effect of training bees to food source at 2000 metres from their hive on the number of visits made by recruits to empty dishes located at various distances from it. (From FRISCH, K. VON, 1967, *The Dance Language and Orientation of Bees*, publisher and copyright as 4–7.)

forager has made a number of successful trips to a water site it exposes its Nasanov scent gland, which is located between the 5th and 6th tergites on the dorsal side of its abdomen (Fig. 1–3), and the pheromone released (which consists of a mixture of geraniol, citral, geranic acid and nerolic acid) attracts potential foragers searching for the site.

Honeybees may also expose their Nasanov glands when foraging at dishes of sugar syrup. However, this is probably in response to an abundant supply of odourless forage usually associated with collecting water, and it is necessary to be cautious when relating communication experiments, in which odourless syrup is used, to communication of natural floral sources. Indeed, the tendencies of foragers to dance and expose their Nasanov glands are not closely related activities, and whereas the presence of an odour at a food source encourages dancing it discourages scenting. Foraging bees may also mark and increase the attractiveness of a food source with a pheromone secreted from glands in their tarsi, but the significance of this behaviour is not yet clear.

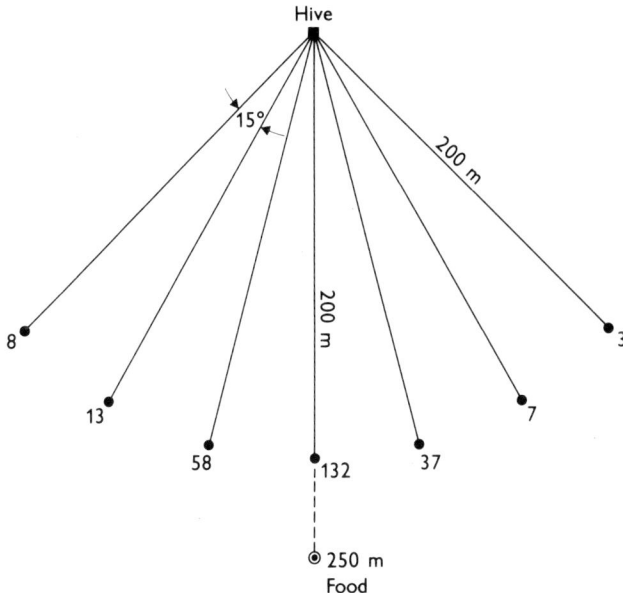

Fig. 4–11 Communication of direction. Effect of training bees to food source on the number of visits made by recruits to empty dishes located at various directions from the hive. (From FRISCH, K. VON, 1950, *Bees: Their Vision, Chemical Senses and Language*, New York, Cornell University Press, and London, Jonathan Cape.)

Bees recruited to a food source may never have visited it before, or may be previously conditioned to it and may have been waiting in the nest until forage from it was again available. Conditioned foragers can be induced to revisit their food source when they are touched by, or when they receive food from, a companion that has just returned from the source but not danced, although a dancing bee is more effective. Conditioned foragers can even be induced to revisit a food source by introducing its odour into their nest. A more primitive form of crop communication also exists because the presence of a particular floral odour in the food stores of a colony can induce foragers that have not visited the source before to do so. Hence the extensive transfer of food that occurs within a colony influences a forager's choice of crop.

Communication of sources of forage helps a colony to function as a single unit, rather than as many independent foragers, and because of chance differences in the crops that different colonies discover, each colony tends to exploit the surrounding flora in a slightly different way. Differences in the floral odour of the food stores of different colonies and in their innate floral preferences reinforce this tendency, and so help to diminish competition between colonies.

5 Queen and Worker Production

5.1 Development and caste determination

Eggs are laid singly on the cell bases and after three days they hatch into larvae. About 125 mg honey and between 70 to 150 mg pollen are required to feed one worker larva, and during its development each receives well over a thousand inspection visits by worker bees and many small feeds (an average of 143 feeds of a total of 109 minutes' duration according to one observer). The number and duration of feeds increases with the larva's age. A nest bee examines a larva intensively before putting brood food on the larva itself, on the cell base, or cell wall near to the larva's mouth.

Queen larvae are fed much more often than worker larvae. It has been estimated that each queen larva receives a total of 1200–1600 feeds of up to 17 hours' total duration.

5.1.1 Larval food

Worker bees feed larvae with a glandular secretion which consists partly of a clear component (mostly protein) from the hypopharyngeal glands and partly of a white component (mostly lipid) from the mandibular glands (Fig 1–3), together with regurgitations from the honeystomach that possibly contain digestive enzymes.

Larvae destined to become queens are fed equal quantities of the above two components throughout their five days of development; this is often known as 'royal jelly'. The composition of royal jelly is incompletely known, but it contains a large amount of the hydroxylated fatty acid 10-hydroxy-*trans*-2-decenoic acid and of the nucleic acids RNA and DNA, together with sugars, proteins, vitamins, amino acids, cholesterol and water.

The glandular secretions fed to larvae destined to become workers consist of 20–40% of the white component for the first two days of larval life, but on the third day the white component ceases to be fed and for the last two days of larval development only the clear glandular secretion is given together with honey, and any pollen it contains. Drone larvae receive more food than worker larvae, but its composition appears to be similar.

It seems likely that a nest bee is able to evaluate the caste and age of a larva and change the proportion and composition of its glandular secretion to suit the one being fed, although the possibility cannot be excluded that the composition of the glandular secretion differs in different workers, and each feeds only those larvae to which its secretion is suited.

Queen cells have a larger diameter than worker cells, and the open end

§ 5.1   DEVELOPMENT AND CASTE DETERMINATION   49

faces downward instead of horizontally. It appears that the worker bees feed a newly hatched larva according to whether it occupies a queen or worker cell, but once differentiation has been established the queen larvae have a greater respiration rate than worker larvae and the category of larva is recognized irrespective of the cell.

5.1.2   *Mechanism of caste differentiation*

Although the differentiation mechanism starts when larvae hatch, it is not complete until after three or more days. A larva up to three days' old can be transferred from a worker to a queen cell and reared as a queen, but the older larvae are when they are transferred, the less strong in the resulting adults are those queen characteristics associated with weight, number of ovarioles, diameter and volume of spermathecae. When larvae between three and four days' old are transferred from worker to queen cells the adults produced have characteristics intermediate between those of workers and queens. Few older larvae survive transference.

The actual mechanism of caste differentiation is still uncertain. It could be the indirect result of difference in nutritional balance acting through the endocrine system of the larvae, or it could be caused by the presence or absence of a labile constituent in one or other diet, or even a difference in the proportion of labile constituent rather than a simple presence or absence. The latest findings suggest that worker larval development is repressed compared with that of queen larvae.

Worker larvae usually move round their cell bases while feeding and average one complete turn in their cells every hour. These movements must help to mix the fresh and old foods together. The large amount of food and care received by each larva is reflected in their extremely rapid growth rate. The weight of the queen larva increases exponentially by a factor of five on each of the first four days after it hatches. Queen larvae always have large amounts of royal jelly available and often much dried food is left uneaten when the larva pupates. In contrast little or none is left in worker cells after pupation.

5.1.3   *Orientation of larvae*

When larval feeding is completed workers build a 'capping' of wax over the open end of the cell and the larva spins its cocoon. After spinning is finished worker and drone larvae invariably face the cell cappings and rest on their dorsal surfaces to complete their development. The stimuli that are primarily responsible for this larval orientation are the rough texture of the capping end wall and the smooth texture of the basal end wall. Worker larvae also respond to the shape of the cell end walls; the capping end is flat and the basal end is round. Cells containing queen larvae that have finished feeding hang downwards, are tubular in cross-section and taper toward their lower capped ends; after the queen larvae have finished spinning they also stretch out longitudinally with their heads toward the capped end of their cells. Queen larvae orientate primarily by gravity, but the rough textured lower end wall is a secondary stimulus. Hence, response to a few simple stimuli ensure that the developing queen, worker or drone is facing the right direction when the time arrives for it to emerge as an adult 16, 21 or 24 days respectively after the egg was laid.

5.2 Queen replacement

The pheromones that have received most study are those emanating from the queen. When a queen moves over the surface of the comb, bees in her path usually back away and so facilitate her progress. When she stops moving, often to examine a cell, bees in the vicinity face toward her forming a circle round her. They frequently examine her with their antennae and sometimes lick her, and by so doing are thought to receive pheromones from her. Those bees near the queen's head may also offer her food. The bees surrounding the queen are constantly changing and few stay for more than a minute.

If a queen is enclosed in filter paper for a few hours the paper attracts the workers as much as did the queen. The pheromones on the queen's body surface can be extracted by solvents, and when they are added to a small piece of pith, plaster of Paris or a dead worker bee, and returned to the hive, they attract a circle of workers in an analogous way to the queen herself.

One of the pheromones that the workers receive is 9-oxo-*trans*-2-decenoic acid. $CH_3CO(CH_2)_5CH:CHCO\cdot OH$, that is produced by the mandibular glands of the queen (Fig. 5–1), discharged at the base of her mandibles, and distributed over her body surface by grooming. In order to compensate for the inactivation of this pheromone within her colony the queen must produce about 5000 µg daily. It has a pronounced effect on inhibiting worker bees from rearing additional queens, although another pheromone from the mandibular glands, 9-hydroxy-*trans*-2-decenoic acid, $CH_3CHOH(CH_2)_5CH:CHCO\cdot OH$, may also contribute toward inhibition. Other, as yet unidentified pheromones are necessary for complete inhibition because a live queen inhibits the rearing of additional queens by colonies more effectively than these two pheromones alone, and even when the manibular glands have been removed from live queens they can still inhibit queen rearing to some extent.

Furthermore the two fatty acids mentioned above are not by themselves able to attract workers. This function is probably served by yet other pheromones that come from the queen's mandibular glands, her Koschevnikov glands which consist of clusters of cells in the sting chamber, and by her dorsal subepidermal abdominal glands.

When a colony loses its queen the workers soon become agitated, readily release pheromones from their Nasanov glands (pages 28 and 46) and

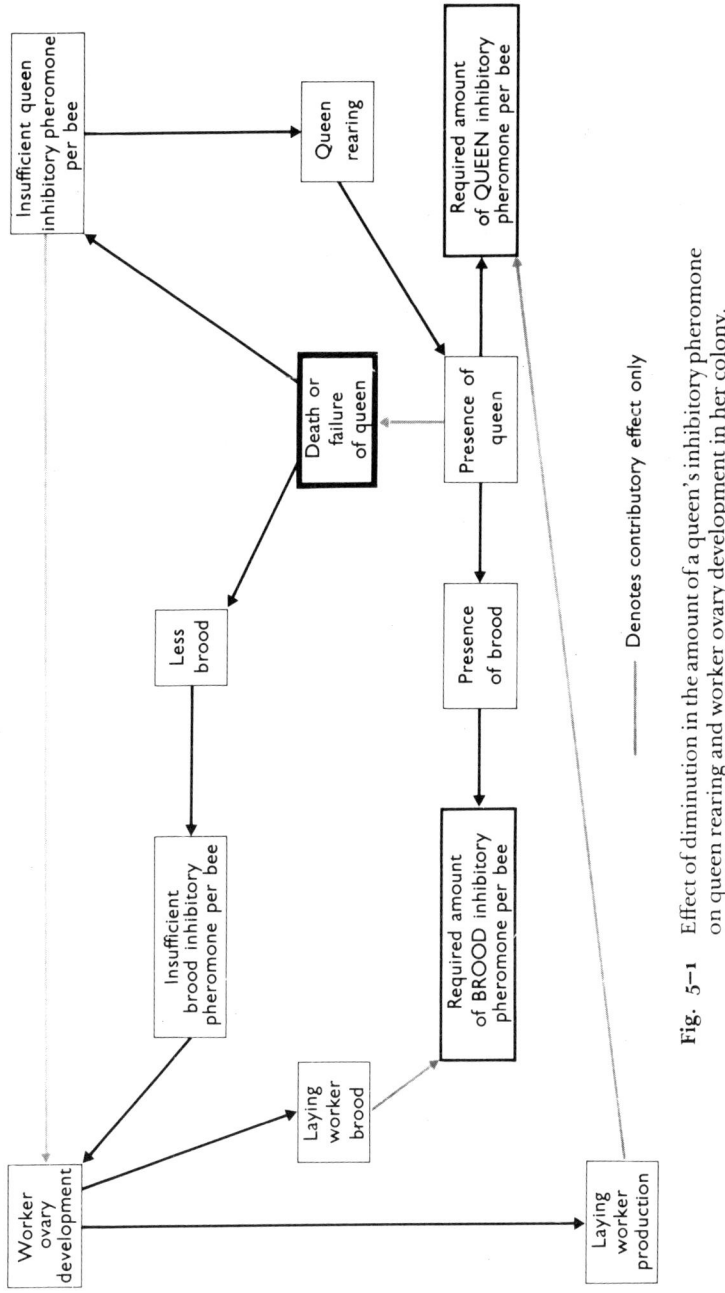

Fig. 5-1 Effect of diminution in the amount of a queen's inhibitory pheromone on queen rearing and worker ovary development in her colony.

disperse them by fanning their wings, as though to attract their queen back to them. Within a few hours to a day or so of the queen being lost the workers have modified some of the existing worker cells, containing female producing eggs and young larvae, so they are larger and project downward from the cell surface. The brood in these 'emergency' queen cells is reared to become replacement queens (page 49). The number of queens reared varies considerably but is usually fewer than ten. Although young larvae are usually available for several days after a queen dies or is removed, on each successive day, fewer queen cells are initiated, indicating that the presence of queen larvae tends to inhibit the production of additional queens.

The first queen to emerge attempts to destroy the others while they are still in their cells. However, often more than one queen manages to emerge and when two meet on the comb they grapple and try to kill each other, until eventually only one of the emerged young queens remains alive. The survivor will tear open any cells that still contain queens, sometimes aided in doing so by the workers. Within a few days the survivor will mate and begin to lay eggs; her full potential in producing inhibiting pheromone is then realized.

In a natural colony the queen is unlikely to disappear abruptly, but as she ages her pheromone production and her inhibitory powers diminish. When her inhibiting influence is no longer adequate the worker bees construct special queen cells that hang from the margin of the comb and in these the queen lays eggs and new queens are reared. Unless the colony swarms (page 54) the ensuing process of queen supersedure is very similar to that following the production of emergency queen cells. The new queen, with her greater pheromone production, effectively inhibits further queen rearing.

The old queen often remains alive until after the surviving young queen has mated and begins laying, sometimes for several weeks. In less efficient cases of supersedure the old queen dies before the young queen emerges, or is killed by the young queen as soon as she is capable of stinging.

5.3 Workers' ovary development

The ovaries of worker bees are normally rudimentary. However, with removal or loss of the queen from a colony the ovaries of some of the workers begin to develop, and about 2 weeks later the ovaries of about half the bees have done so. Young nest bees develop their ovaries more quickly than older bees, but workers of all ages may eventually do so. Worker bees that were reared in queenless colonies have an increased tendency to develop their ovaries. However, only a small percentage of bees with developed ovaries lay eggs; they do so for relatively short periods only and between times continue their normal duties.

Hence development of workers' ovaries does not occur until a

§5.3 WORKERS' OVARY DEVELOPMENT

considerable time after a colony has become queenless and after queen production has been initiated. Pheromones from the queen contribute toward inhibition of worker ovary development, and the presence of a few workers with developed ovaries in some, but not other, colonies with a queen is probably related to the amount of queen pheromone produced. However, volatile pheromones produced by worker brood are primarily responsible for inhibition of worker ovary development, pheromones from pupae being as effective as pheromones from larvae. Therefore the brood remaining in a colony after the queen is lost temporarily suppresses ovary development until a new queen is reared.

Even in a queenless colony without brood, the chaos and disorganization that would result from each worker reproducing independently is avoided as laying workers themselves produce pheromones that help to inhibit ovary development. This, together with the discovery that brood produced from laying worker eggs is as effective in inhibiting ovary development as brood produced from a queen's eggs, helps explain why the proportion of workers with enlarged ovaries in a colony is always limited. The increased grooming that occurs in queenless colonies may help to distribute pheromones.

Although many bees with developed ovaries are frequently examined and mauled by others in a queenless colony, in a similar manner to that in which guard bees react toward intruders (page 34), some laying workers are especially attractive to other bees which lick and examine them and sometimes form a circle round them as if they were queens. Such 'false queens' mostly do no worker duties, and they appear especially effective in discouraging ovary development in, and egg-laying by, other workers.

Eggs produced by laying workers are haploid and produce males only. Although laying workers prefer to lay in drone cells, in contrast to the queen they readily lay haploid eggs in worker cells. Their activities help to ensure a supply of drones to mate with any queen that is eventually produced.

6 Colony Reproduction

6.1 Swarming

The honeybee colony reproduces by swarming. There is normally only one queen in a honeybee colony, but before swarming the colony rears additional queens. The old queen, and a proportion of the workers and drones usually leave the hive and fly off in a well defined group or swarm when the new queens are in the pupal stage. They usually soon settle and form a temporary cluster on a suitable support such as a branch of a tree where they remain from a few hours to a few days, before again flying off together to a new home where they build comb and rear brood. Some of the replacement queens that are reared by the parent colony in their old hive may leave with other swarms during the next week or so, but one young queen remains behind in the parent colony, mates and lays eggs.

6.1.1 The swarming process

In the initial stages of swarm preparation and instability of the colony, nest bees become reluctant to accept the nectar loads of foragers and foraging diminishes. Some of the redundant foragers search for a suitable nest site for the swarm.

The nest bees also cease to feed the queen who lays progressively fewer eggs until she stops altogether and her abdomen shrinks. By the time her colony swarms she has lost about a third of her weight; presumably she would otherwise find difficulty in flying. The decreased foraging and brood rearing in a colony before swarming results in an increase in the development of the hypopharyngeal glands and ovaries of the worker bees; perhaps these enlarged organs may serve as protein stores.

The emergence of the swarm usually occurs a day or so before the first of the queens being reared emerges from her cell. It is preceded and associated with 'buzzing runs' by the workers; while performing these the bees run in straight lines across the comb, at the same time vibrating their partially spread wings every 0.5 to 3.0 seconds with a frequency of 180 to 250 cycles per second. They frequently touch other bees, and maintain contact with them for up to 5 seconds while buzzing their wings at 400–500 cycles per second. The bees contacted also start buzzing runs so the disturbance and excitement rapidly multiplies and soon leads to the emergence of the bees as a swarm.

Although most of the bees of a colony initially leave with the swarm many return again, and the swarm that moves off contains about half the original population. The factors determining which bees go with the swarm are unknown. Worker bees are attracted to the sight, sound and odours of each other, but pheromones produced from the queen's mandibular glands and from the workers' Nasanov glands are most important in co-ordinating swarm movement and in maintaining swarm cohesion.

A swarm in the air is strongly attracted to its queen and will fly as a cohesive unit only if the queen is with it; the pheromone 9-oxo-*trans*-2-decenoic acid seems to be primarily responsible for this cohesion but others may also be involved. However, scout bees guide an airborne swarm by releasing their Nasanov gland pheromone while flying and when they land at the clustering site, and the swarm begins to cluster while the queen is still in the air. Synthetic Nasanov gland pheromone can be used to guide a swarm, but only if the queen is present to maintain its cohesion. Should a swarm lose its queen after it has settled, it soon disperses and returns home. However, if she is merely misplaced, her pheromones enable the bees to quickly locate and rejoin her. Experiments have shown that the bees of a swarm are able to distinguish their own from 'foreign' queens. When the workers find and recognize their *own* queen they feed her and dispense Nasanov gland pheromone and so attract the rest of the swarm. When they find a 'foreign' queen they may be antagonistic to her and signal her rejection by marking her with alarm pheromones (page 30).

Once settled on a branch the bees of a swarm form a cluster with a compact covering of about 3 bees thick of the older bees and a loosely packed interior of younger bees. An entrance hole into the interior is clearly defined an hour or two after the settling of the swarm.

The average amount of food present in the honeystomachs of the nest-bees increases four or five fold during the 10 days before a colony swarms, so that the bees of the swarm take with them a reserve of food. Most bees in the swarm cluster remain quiescent and their food decreases only slowly and steadily, although the loads of a minority of bees that search actively for the final nest site, rapidly diminish.

When one of these scout bees discovers a suitable permanent nest site it performs a dance on the side of the swarm cluster by which it indicates the direction and distance of the site, in a similar manner to which successful foragers indicate the location of a food source (page 42). Periodically the scout bee returns to the potential nest site and marks it with Nasanov gland pheromone. The dances stimulate other bees to visit the nest site and they may also dance on their return.

In the initial stages of nest site selection scout bees dancing on the cluster surface may indicate two or more different potential sites. However, the more vigorous and persistent dancers recruit more followers and even obtain converts from those dancing less vigorously, so that usually competition is gradually and democratically eliminated and more and more dancers agree to the same location; when they all do so the swarm leaves for the selected nest site. If the choice is otherwise equal a more distant site tends to be favoured; this obviously helps to lessen competition between the parent colony and the swarm for available forage.

Although complete agreement of the scouts is usual it is not a prerequisite for swarm departure, and occasionally a swarm departs while the scouts are still indicating different potential nest sites. However, it is necessary for sufficient scouts to be aware of the chosen location to guide the swarm successfully to it.

The departure of the swarm from its temporary site to its permanent home is again initiated by 'buzzing runs' and once airborne it is again guided by release of Nasanov gland pheromone by the scout bees and maintained as a coherent whole by pheromones released from the queen's mandibular glands. When the swarm has settled in its new site the honey carried in the bees' honeystomachs provide the source of energy and wax for establishing the colony. The bees begin to forage, and the queen rapidly increases in weight and begins to lay eggs.

If the parental colony does not swarm again the first virgin queen to emerge from its cell disposes of its rivals in the same manner as when an old queen is being superseded. If, however, one or more additional swarms emerge, each with a virgin queen, they are often preceded by queen 'piping'. The first virgin queen to emerge produces this piping sound by contracting its flight muscles with its wings still folded which produces a frequency of vibration of 435 to 493 cycles per second (double that produced with the wings spread). At the same time she presses her thorax against the comb surface, which communicates the vibration to the comb and hence to the legs of other bees through which it is received. The queens still in their cells respond by a quacking sound of 323 cycles per second. It is believed that one or both sounds cause the worker bees to delay the emergence of the remaining virgins from their cells, and so prevent mortal combat, but they probably also help stimulate the colony to swarm. When a colony has ceased producing swarms, the workers allow the first virgin that emerges to destroy the remainder.

6.1.2 Factors causing swarming

Migration or absconding differs from swarming in that (a) the *entire* colony moves to a new location in response to unsatisfactory conditions in the nest or the environment, and (b) it is not associated with queen rearing (Fig. 6–1). Migration is extremely common among *A. mellifera, A. cerana, A. dorsata* and *A. florea* in tropical countries. It is rare or absent among *A. mellifera* colonies in temperate countries.

In contrast queen rearing is associated with the early stages of both swarming and supersedure (Fig. 6–1), although the factors that decide whether a colony swarms or merely supersedes its queen are still not clear. It would appear that swarming, like supersedure is often initiated by queen pheromone deficiency. This is supported by findings that colonies

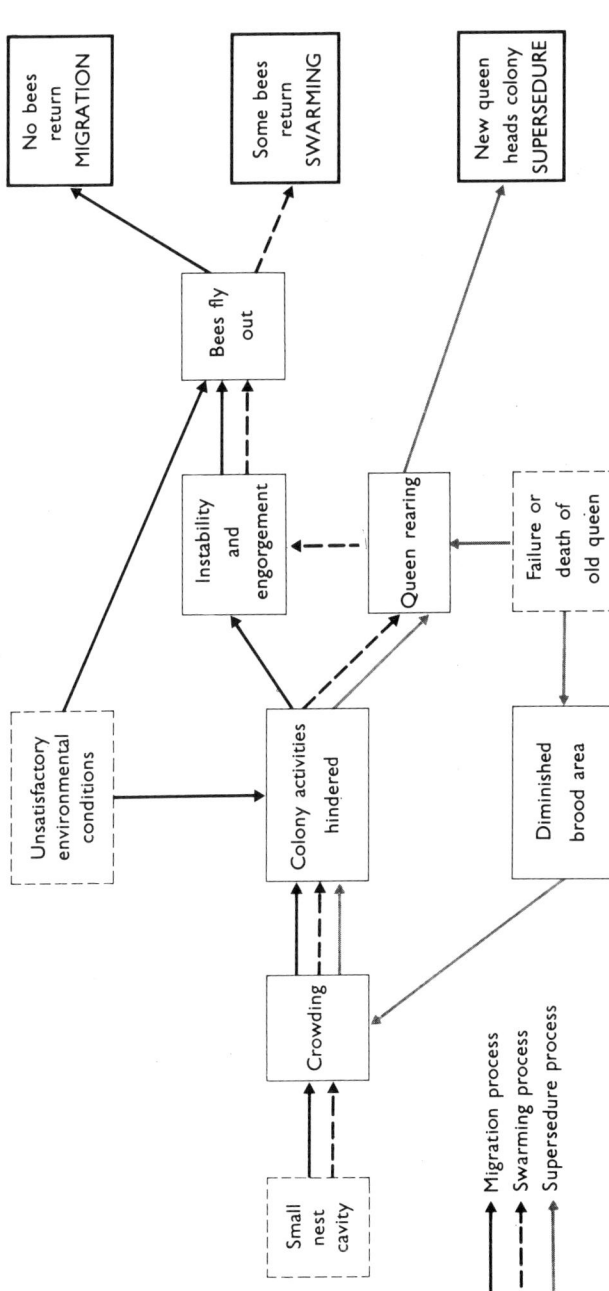

Fig. 6-1 Processes leading to migration, swarming or supersedure. (Adapted from Simpson, J., 1974, Report of the Central Association of Beekeepers.)

headed by queens of the current year are less likely to swarm than those headed by older queens, whose pheromone production is declining. Furthermore, the queen of a swarm is often herself superseded within a few months. It seems that a seasonal cycle may be involved in determining whether in a colony with queen pheromone deficiency, swarming or supersedure occurs.

In temperate climates the peak production of queen cells, in common with that of worker and drone brood, occurs in mid-summer. However, swarms need several weeks to become established and build an adequate food reserve for unfavourable seasons, and the maximum incidence of swarming occurs in late spring to early summer; for example in New York State about 80% of swarms emerge between mid-May and mid-July.

Supersedure occurs most often just before or just after the period when swarming is most frequent. Any supersedure that coincides with the main swarming period probably occurs in small colonies, or in colonies whose workers have a small requirement for inhibiting pheromone.

The causes of this swarming cycle are unknown but they are probably associated with various physiological changes in the worker bees, including changes in the state of the fat bodies and hypopharyngeal glands during the summer. Indeed, there may be differences in the proportion of bees of the same age but different physiological conditions that leave with a swarm.

It is well established that the crowding of bees which occurs when a colony became too large for its nest space, can cause swarming, even when no queen cells have been built. Crowding could hinder queen pheromone collection and distribution; when an uncrowded colony makes swarm preparations the brood area diminishes and the density of bees on it increases and so produces a similar effect.

The tendency of a colony to swarm or to supersede may also be partly genetically determined. Beekeepers in temperate countries deliberately or inadvertently select for colonies that do not swarm so perhaps most colonies of *A. mellifera* that have been studied swarm less than their predecessors.

6.2 Drone production

In temperate climates most honeybee colonies produce drones during spring and summer and at the end of the summer drones are evicted from the nest by workers.

The queen honeybee possesses a muscular mechanism at the opening of her spermatheca whereby only a few sperm cells at a time are allowed to leave and fertilize eggs about to be laid. If the eggs are fertilized (diploid) they develop into females. If they are not fertilized (haploid) they develop into drones.

However, recent work has confirmed that the genes at the female-

§ 6.2   DRONE PRODUCTION   59

determining locus must be heterozygous, as is normally so, to produce diploid females. If they are homozygous, as frequently occurs in artificially inbred colonies diploid *male* eggs are produced and laid in worker cells. But soon after these diploid male eggs become larvae they are eaten by workers, and so even in these abnormal circumstances the production of excess males is prevented.

6.2.1 *Discrimination of cell types*

Male-producing eggs are laid in larger cells (drone cells 6.2 to 7.0 mm diameter) than worker-producing eggs (worker cells 5.3 to 6.3 mm diameter). When a choice of cells is available the queen will often lay several consecutive eggs that have all been fertilized (in worker cells) or all unfertilized (in drone cells). It is not known whether she rejects the other type of cell (i.e. the type of egg, fertilized or unfertilized, determines the type of cell selected) or whether only one type of cell has been prepared by the workers to receive eggs (i.e. the laying of fertilized or unfertilized eggs is determined by the type of cell available).

Queens that have no sperm, either because they have not been fertilized, or because their supply is exhausted, do not prefer drone cells; hence, either they are no longer able to discriminate between the two types of cell, or, more likely, they are unaware that the eggs they lay in worker cells are not fertilized.

Workers with developed ovaries (page 52) prefer to lay their eggs (always unfertilized) in drone cells, but in contrast to fertilized queens they readily do so in worker cells.

It is unlikely that bees distinguish the different types of cells by their size and orientation alone. It appears that a queen's normal response to a cell is to lay a fertilized egg, and that drone cells produce specific stimuli that prevent the laying of fertilized eggs. The odour of the drone comb which differs from that of worker comb seems to be the prime stimulus, and the queen confirms the presence of a drone cell by measuring its width with her front legs. If the queen's legs are amputated or small projecting flaps of cellulose tape fixed to them, the queen is unable to confirm her identification and mostly lays fertilized instead of unfertilized eggs in drone cells.

6.2.2 *Drone cell production*

The presence of a queen stimulates the production of workers, probably by a pheromone from her mandibular glands, but drone rearing is only possible in a colony if it has drone cells. Many beekeepers regard drone production as wasteful and attempt to avoid having any drone comb in the brood areas of colonies. However, under natural conditions colonies build many drone cells, and the amount built by newly established swarms or colonies deprived of their combs is determined by the colonies' need to rear drone brood.

Bees of a swarm or combless colony, build only worker cells at first and later tend to build drone cells, so that in colonies established within hollow trees and other sheltered cavities, the drone cells tend to be located toward the edge and bases of the few large combs. During winter the bees of a colony withdraw from the cells at the outsides of the combs, and as they become more populous the following spring, spread out to occupy them again, and if necessary to build more comb. The amount of drone comb built by a combless colony, or an expanding colony with space to build, depends on the size of the population and the time of year. Small colonies build a smaller proportion of drone to worker comb than large colonies, and colonies, with less than about 6000 bees do not build drone comb at all. In England the total amount of comb constructed is greater in May and June than the rest of the year, and the proportion of drone cells built is greatest in May, June and July.

Large colonies may continue to build drone cells long after the rearing of drone brood has ceased for the year; hence the construction of drone cells and the rearing of drones are not always controlled by the same mechanism.

The amount of drone comb built in a colony also depends on the amount already present which somehow over-rides the effect of the time of the year in determining drone cell production. Colonies without drone comb build a greater proportion of drone cells and more drone cells per bee, than colonies with drone comb. It is difficult to understand how the bees know how many drone cells are in their colony, unless a pheromone is incorporated into them as they are built.

The mechanism controlling cell building is not fully understood, and it is not even known whether individual bees change freely between building one kind of cell to the other. However, the mechanism appears to act primarily in determining what kind of cell base is built, and once the bases of drone cells have been laid their completion is probable. If, as seems likely, worker and drone cells have different scents, this would greatly facilitate the work of the building bees.

In extreme circumstances modifications are made. If colonies are only given a nest of drone combs the bees add wax to the cell walls until their internal dimensions approximate to those of worker cells. In spring, colonies deprived by beekeepers of drone comb will often build it in any space available in their hives, even destroying worker cells at the corners of comb in order to make room for it.

6.2.3 Drone brood production

When drone production is limited by shortage of drone comb, much of the drone comb built is used immediately for rearing brood. In these circumstances it is probable that the building of drone comb and the rearing of drone brood are governed by similar factors. But when colonies have ample drone comb available the amount of drone brood reared is positively correlated with the amount of worker brood (Fig. 6–2) and with the adult bee population for colonies of up to about 10 000 bees; thereafter there is no increase with the numbers of bees present. Removing drone brood from colonies encourages its production and adding drone brood to colonies diminishes its production.

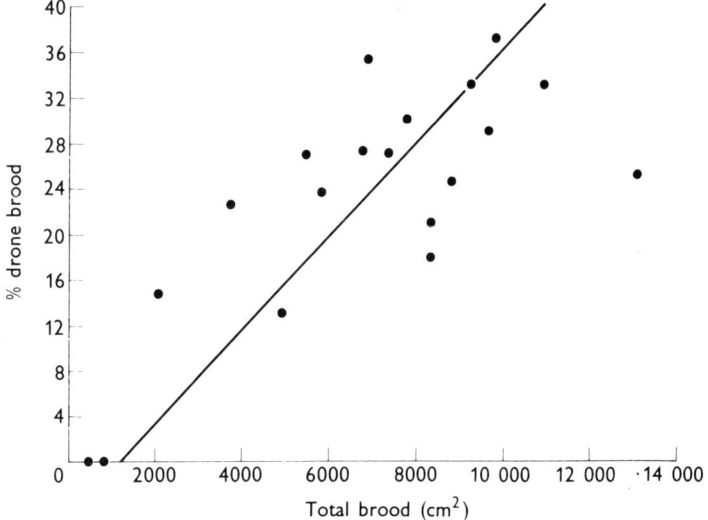

Fig. 6–2 Relationship between the amount of brood present in colonies in May and the proportion of it that was drone. (After Free, J. B. and Williams, Ingrid H., 1975, *Anim. Behav.*, **23**, 650–75.)

Small colonies have a greater proportion of brood, especially drone brood, in the egg stage, than large colonies. This suggests that the queens are laying more eggs than their workers can rear and the workers regulate the amount of brood by destroying or eating some of the eggs or young larvae.

Such regulation is particularly prevalent early in the season, and in colonies with ample drone comb a large percentage of eggs are sometimes laid in drone cells before the end of April, although few are reared. The peak time of drone production varies with location. In England the number of drones being reared and the drone to worker ratio reaches a peak in May and June (Fig. 6–3) and few eggs are laid in drone cells after July. The peak production in Scotland occurs from mid-June to late July.

6.2.4 *Drone behaviour*

Drones fertilize the virgin queen, but except for inadvertently helping to regulate temperature, have no other function. Whilst inside the nest

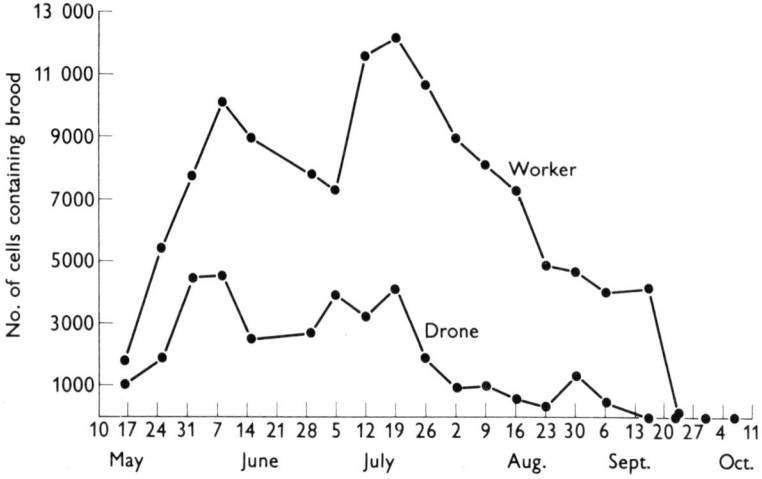

Fig. 6-3 The production of worker and drone brood in a colony at different times of the year. Fluctuations in weather conditions and available forage produce fluctuations in brood production. (After Free, J. B. and Williams, Ingrid H., 1975, *Anim. Behav.*, **23**, 650-75.

they spend nearly three-quarters of their time in periods of apparent inactivity which are frequently broken by periods of movement over the comb.

For the first few days of their lives, drones receive their food direct from workers that are producing brood food. However, as they become older they are fed less by workers and when about a week old they obtain all their food directly from honey cells. Drones are particularly prone to feed themselves either just before or just after they have flown from their nest.

6.2.5 Drone eviction

The eviction of drones is seldom a rapid process; indeed before drones are evicted they are often denied access to food so that they become too weak to fly. The workers cling to the drones, pulling and chewing their wings and legs (Fig. 6.4). The attacked drone often adopts a 'flinching posture' in which it contracts its legs on one side and outstretches them on the other, at the same time turning its head away from the attacker. When the attack has ceased the drone runs off, and may even attempt to do so with the worker still clinging to it if the attack is long and severe.

The behaviour of workers toward a drone appears to be associated with his age. At the same time as some of the older drones are being attacked by workers, the younger drones present in the brood combs are still being fed.

Fig. 6–4 A drone being evicted from its hive by two worker bees.

The most important factor initiating the seasonal rejection of drones seems to be a reduction in the amount of forage being collected. An abrupt change in the supply of forage produces a more marked response than a gradual one. At any time of the year a colony can be caused to evict its drones by preventing it from foraging, or by the onset of dearth conditions.

However, at times of year when little forage is available, no drones are evicted by colonies without mated laying queens, which helps to ensure a supply of drones to mate with any new queens produced. In such colonies eviction begins soon after the virgin queens have mated and laid eggs.

6.2.6 Regulating mechanisms

The production of drone comb and brood and the toleration of adult drones seems to be regulated by the balance of pro-drone factors (P) and anti-drone factors (A).

Probably a laying queen produces factor A that inhibits the rearing of drone brood and tolerance of drones. Factor P appears to be associated largely with the quantity of forage being collected, perhaps directly so in some circumstances such as the effect of an abrupt end to foraging on drone eviction, but also directly or indirectly on the amount of brood that is reared. It seems that the relative strengths of factors A and P determine the proportion of drone cells built, the amount of drone brood reared and the attitude of workers toward drones (Fig. 6–5). Thus, the reluctance of colonies to build drone comb in early spring when their worker

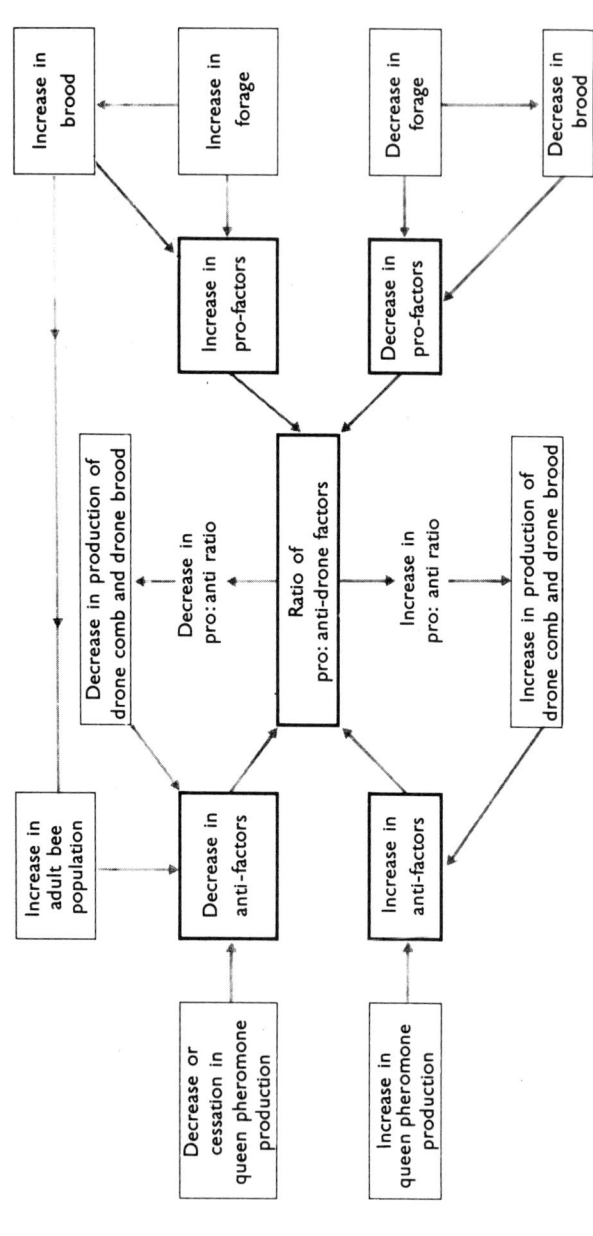

Fig. 6–5 Summary of the factors that contribute toward (pro-drone) and against (anti-drone) the production of drone comb and drone brood.

§ 6.3   MATING   65

populations are relatively small, and the reluctance of small colonies to build drone comb at any time suggest that the amount of factor A produced by a queen is sufficient to inhibit drone cell production, but that as a colony becomes larger and the amount of factor A circulating among the bees is attenuated, inhibition is no long complete. Furthermore, early in the season the small amount of brood that is present in a colony produces insufficient factor P to neutralize factor A, but as the amount of worker brood (and factor P) increases there is also an increase in the proportion of drone brood reared. Toward the end of the summer, as brood rearing decreases, the queen's factor A reasserts its influence. When a queen is removed from a colony drone cells are built only if brood (factor P) is present.

Gradual or abrupt changes in the tendency of workers to evict drones can be explained by gradual or abrupt changes in the proportion of P and A. Thus an abrupt end to foraging (factor P) hastens eviction, whereas removal of the queen (factor A) delays it.

Drone cell production, drone rearing and the tolerance of drones by workers is encouraged in the presence of failing queens, with a diminished output of pheromone, and presumably also of factor A, if the two are distinct. Foragers are less likely than nest bees to receive that part of factor P emanating from the brood, which helps explain why older drones may be attacked by unemployed foragers while younger drones of the same colony are being fed by the workers.

It is probable that drone comb and drone brood also produce factor A; this would account for the feed-back mechanism whereby when sufficient drone comb or brood is present further production is inhibited (Fig. 6–3).

6.3 Mating

6.3.1 Mating flights

Mating flights of drones and virgin queens occur mostly on warm sunny afternoons with wind speeds of less than 20 km per hour. They are of 10 to 55 minutes duration for drones and 5 to 20 minutes for queens. Drones begin to make mating flights when one to two weeks old. The queens usually mate when 3 to 16 days old and if they have failed to do so by the time they are three or four weeks old they cease to make mating flights and lay unfertilized eggs only.

During a successful mating flight a queen may mate up to ten times in quick succession. If she returns home with insufficient sperm in her spermatheca she makes a subsequent mating flight a day or so later.

Mating is quick and violent. During it the distal portion of the drone penis is explosively everted into the open sting chamber of the queen, and is broken off when the drone disengages. He subsequently dies, so it is only unsuccessful males that return home from mating flights.

6.3.2 Drone congregation areas

In many regions there are special mating areas, known as drone congregation areas, that are used for several years in succession. These drone congregation areas are likely to occur in hilly or mountainous country, but they may be absent in flat, featureless country. However, the factors that determine their location are not fully understood.

The limits of a congregation area vary with the number and flight intensity of the drones. The drones may come from a catchment area of 260 to 520 km² and so provide considerable genetic variability. When a queen enters a drone congregation area she is soon mated. The further she mates from her hive, the greater the probability that new gene combinations will result.

6.3.3 Mating process

Studies of the mating process have made considerable progress recently because of the discovery that drones are attracted to virgin queens that are suspended from helium filled balloons or elevated poles. The queens are attractive at heights 6 to 15 metres above ground; the lowest height at which they are attractive varies inversely with the wind speed.

A drone first perceives a virgin queen by the odour of her mandibular gland secretion when about 50 metres from her. The drone's sense organs that respond to the mandibular gland secretion are located primarily in his antennae. He reacts by moving toward the source of the odour and a 'comet' of hundreds of males may form below a single queen. A drone can first see a queen when about 1 metre from her and before attempting to mate he examines her with his antennae and front legs.

It is possible to simulate virgin queens by wooden models coated with mandibular gland secretion. Copulation can be obtained if the model is provided with an orifice of similar size and depth to the open sting chamber.

The mandibular gland secretion of *Apis cerana, dorsata* and *florea* queens also attracts *A. mellifera* drones. The pheromone 9-oxo-*trans*-2-decenoic acid is the main component of the mandibular gland secretion that is involved (9-hydroxy-*trans*-2-decenoic acid is of secondary importance). Thus the same pheromone, 9-oxo-*trans*-2-decenoic acid, has two different functions depending upon circumstances; inside the nest it helps inhibit reproduction (page 50) and in the field it encourages it. Furthermore, while in the nest drones ignore queens.

Other pheromones may act as aphrodisiacs or stimulate mounting and copulation.

7 Conclusions

It has become increasingly apparent that the activities of the members of a colony are related to colony needs, but the mechanisms by which adjustments are made are far from understood. Much research needs to be done before it is known why a particular bee does a particular task, and how the actions of the thousands of physically independent but physiologically dependent individuals are welded together to make a colony function as a coherent whole.

But already it is clear that much of the behaviour is regulated by pheromones that are produced by adult and immature stages of queens, workers and drones, as well as being incorporated into the comb. For example, it appears that pheromones produced by worker brood stimulate pollen collection, inhibit the development of workers' ovaries, and encourage drone production. Pheromones produced by the queen inhibit the rearing of queens, and stimulate building of worker comb, cell cleaning, brood rearing, foraging, honey storage, and pollen deposition. It is indeed coming increasingly apparent that one of the principal functions of a queen is to stimulate the activities of her worker bees.

Much of the seasonal regulation of the activities of the honeybee colony can be explained by the extent to which the pheromones produced by the queen honeybee become distributed among the members of her colony. The greater amount of pheromone distributed per bee in small colonies explains why they rear relatively more brood than large colonies, and why they have a greater stimulus to forage; this increased activity is obviously very important in inducing the rapid growth of swarms and small colonies so they reach sufficient size with sufficient stores to survive the winter.

Most pheromones whose function is known, at least to some extent, remain to be chemically identified, and probably many more, particularly ones concerned with communicative activities such as larval feeding, crop location and clustering, remain to be discovered.

Eventually it is hoped that by providing appropriate chemical and behavioural stimuli it will be possible to programme a colony's activities so its value in crop pollination and honey production will be enhanced.

Further Reading

DADANT and SON (1975), *The Hive and the Honey Bee*. Hamilton, Illinois, Dadant & Son.

FREE, J. B. (1970). *Insect Pollination of Crops*. London, Academic Press.

FRISCH, KARL VON (1967). *The Dance Language and Orientation of Bees*. London, Oxford University Press.

MICHENER, C. D. (1974). *The Social Behaviour of the Bees*. Cambridge, Massachusetts, Harvard University Press.

WILSON, E. O. (1971). *The Insect Societies*. Cambridge, Massachusetts, Harvard University Press.

Printed in Great Britain
by Amazon

Thank You for purchasing

If you liked this book, we welcome your comments!

Visit

www.StevenDavidLampley.com

and tell us what you thought!*

*Submitting a comment signifies your approval for your comment to be used in future
marketing of books, publications, websites, or other promotional efforts.

He received two awards for Police Officer of the Year as well as numerous departmental and civilian commendations.

Steven now uses his experience as an author writing true crime, police, and crime horror fiction and is also an actor accepting police and crime roles for television and film. Steven serves as a police advisor for film and actors on police procedure.

He also speaks to police and corrections academies, high schools, colleges and universities, and organizations on a variety of topics including how to catch a liar, developing mental toughness, forensics, serial killers, crime, and related topics.

• • • • •

To have Steven speak at your high school,
college or university, police or corrections academy,
corporation, or organization,
make contact through
Steven's website:

www.StevenDavidLampley.com

ABOUT THE AUTHOR

Steven wasn't always a police officer. He was a banker and real estate appraiser before his police career. Giving up the corporate world, he applied to the Birmingham (Alabama) Police Department and was accepted to the police academy. Steven spent twenty-one years in a career as police officer and SVU detective. Steven was friends with Jeffrey Dahmer (serial killer and cannibal) and was the arresting officer of The Clairemont Killer (serial killer) featured on America's Most Wanted® and case coverage on such television networks as Investigation Discovery®, The Discovery Channel®, and TruTV® as well as the New York Times® and Los Angeles Times®.

Steven developed, implemented, and supervised a new Special Victim's Unit (SVU) criminal investigative division centered on internet sex crimes. Steven was the arresting officer of a Fugitive from Justice and Canada's Most Wanted and worked closely with the FBI, DOJ United States Attorney's Office, United States Postal Inspector's Service, and Alabama Attorney General's office.

09

The rifling of a gun barrel is what gives the firearm its class characteristics.

A vehicle collision has various parts that may include all or part of the following:

1. First possible perception point
2. Actual perception point
3. No escape point
4. Operator action point
5. Initial engagement point
6. Final rest position

Two ways to identify a cigarette butt from a crime scene:

1. Using the Fire Safety Compliant cigarettes (required in the United States), each cigarette is required to have fire retardant bands to slow the burn rate of a cigarette. The difference in the characteristics (width of the individual bands and their spacing from each other) can help identify the manufacturer and, subsequently, the brand of cigarette.

2. Using the plug wrap from filtered cigarettes. The plug wrap is utilized in a cigarette to enclose the filter. A forensic expert can use the wrap and the adhesive used to secure the wrap as a means of identifying the cigarette manufacturer.

If a human hair is found on a crime scene, a forensic experts can tell what part of the body the hair is from.

Types of Evidence:

1. Associative: Evidence linking a person to a crime.
2. Biological: Evidence from animals, plants, or humans.
3. Impression: Evidence made from an object being imprinted into another object.
4. Reconstructive: Evidence that allows a detective to reconstruct the crime.
5. Trace: Small amounts of evidence typically left behind as a result of a transfer of materials.
6. Transient: Evidence that will erode if not preserved.

Using footprints to determining the body weight of an individual is called Barefoot Morphology.

The length of time after death is called the Postmortem Interval.

After a bullet is fired, it can take as long as ten minutes for the airborne residual gunshot residue to settle.

Hair is predominantly composed of keratin.

A large number of serial killers admit to having an abnormally strong sex drive.

The same type of skin cells make up the mouth as make up the vagina.

If a suspect is located during the investigation, (s)he is not allowed to return to the crime scene to prevent crime scene contamination.

The femur, the largest bone in the human body, can support thirty times the weight of an individual's body.

Chain of Custody of evidence is a process by which evidence is tracked from possession from person to person.

It keeps track of the evidence so that there is no opportunity for the evidence to be tampered with.

Physical evidence of animals, humans, or vegetation is called Biological Evidence.

Bullet wounds typically have soot around the entry point.

A Serum Stain is a stain that is the result of the serum of the blood separating during the process of coagulation.

Most serial killers experienced child abuse.

When working undercover, police do not have to identify themselves as police officers when asked.

There is no way to sober up quickly. Coffee, cold showers, or vomiting will not help.

A forensic document examiner has to obtain sample handwriting made at approximately the same time as the questioned document as young people are still developing their handwriting style and older individuals may show signs of writing deterioration.

Typically, individuals burn approximately 0.016 percent of their blood alcohol content every hour.

Blood spatter can be used to determine if there was a struggle.

Law enforcement frequently receive unrealistic and undeliverable demands that they produce forensics results that the person has seen on a forensics show on television.

Females are better at picking out smells than men.

Fingerprint arches represent approximately five percent of the population's fingerprint patterns.

When analyzing a bullet shot from a firearm, the forensic expert will look at lands and grooves that leave impressions on that bullet. A land is the indented portion of the bullet (the raised portion of the firearm).

Offender profiling is not to pick out a single suspect but to help narrow the field of suspects.

A majority of deaths in a fire occur, not because of the fire itself causing the death, but because of a lack of breathable oxygen.

A Mass Murderer is someone who kills at least four people within a twenty-four hour time frame.

More mass shootings occur with the suspect using pistols (approximately sixty percent).

Iris scans are more accurate than DNA.

Serial killer, John Wayne Gacy, painted pictures in prison and these paintings sold for as much as $20,000.

A powder (smokeless) that is composed of both nitrocellulose and nitroglycerine is called a Double Base.

Felony trials have an approximate eighty-five percent conviction rate.

A hair has three different parts:
1. Cuticle – the outside sheath made up of scales.
2. Cortex – the thickest portion of the hair arranges in a regular pattern of cells. Responsible for the moisture content of the hair.
3. Medulla – a 'central canal' middle of the hair. Determines the color of hair.

The bacterial digestion of the remains of a human body is called Putrefaction.

Regarding serial killers, a Buffer Zone is the area between the serial killer's base and the areas of his murders.

A Folie a Deux is a lust killing with a female suspect with a male accomplice.

Of all felony charges approximately eleven percent are reduced to misdemeanors.

Blood pattern wipe occurs when blood already on a surface is swiped by another object.

Jacketed bullets are typically ten percent zinc and ninety percent copper.

Indicators of arson:
1. Multiple locations of ignition
2. Lines of accelerant residue
3. Presence of unburned accelerants
4. Most fire damage having taken place at the floor level.

Whether or not a person is accepted by the court as an expert witness is up to the judge.

The spree and mass murderer are not concerned with who they kill. Anyone who is in their path is subject to being killed.

PBX is a plastic, flexible explosive.

While there are two dichotomies of serial killer crime scenes, Organized or Disorganized, a crime scene can be Mixed. A mixed crime scene can exist for several reasons. Two of those reasons is that the serial killer is morphing from one of the other category or the serial killer was taken by surprise during his crime and forced him to divert from his normal routine.

A blood alcohol level of 0.25 or over can be deadly.

Vehicle crashes occur in three parts:

1. Pre-Impact
2. Impact
3. Post Impact

The 'spokes' sticking outward from a blood drop are called spines.

SICAR is the Shoeprint Image Capture and Retrieval system for linking footwear impressions left on a crime scene. This system links to more than three hundred footwear manufacturers.

Most children experiment with fire play but that normally subsides by the time they reach puberty.

Serial killer Leonarda Cianciulli, made soap out of her victims.

A forensic document examiner can differentiate between the natural differences in a suspect's handwriting versus different writers that may be of similar handwriting.

Of all arsons, only about seventeen percent result in the apprehension of a suspect.

month, with a cooling-off period between murders.

Most arsonists have an IQ in the seventy to ninety range.

Charles Scott Robinson was convicted of six counts of rape (child) and was sentenced to 30,000 years in prison.

A Bullet Wipe is the ring shaped found around the bullet entrance wound and is made up of gunshot residue.

Approximately thirty-five percent of psychopaths have abnormal patterns in their brainwaves.

Evidence that can be traced to a single source is called individual evidence.

A person's hearing decreases if (s)he eats too much.

The firing pin pattern on an empty bullet casing can change over time on the same gun.

Handwriting analysis is based on the premise that each person has a unique handwriting style.

Approximately ninety percent of all arsons are committed by white males.

If an individual's body core temperature reaches approximately 107.6°, heatstroke may not be able to be reversed and may cause death.

Most cartridge cases are composed of seventy percent copper and thirty percent zinc.

Fewer home burglaries occur in February than any other month.

Maggots should be preserved in seventy percent ethyl or isopropyl alcohol for forensic processing.

Approximately thirty percent of American's have been arrested by the time they reach twenty-three years of age.

Arsonists are typically nocturnal individuals.

Once a bullet reaches approximately 1,200 feet per second, a mushrooming takes place on its nose.

Homicide victims on a crime scene are not covered until all evidence is gathered.

The definition of a serial killer is someone who has murdered three or more people over a period of more than a

Under normal conditions, if a deceased is warm and not stiff the approximate time of death is less than three hours previous.

Most people hear between ten to over two hundred lies each day.

Beetles typically appear on a deceased body after five to eleven days.

A Grand Jury's purpose is to hear evidence and decide if evidence is sufficient to formally accuse someone of a crime.

Detectives may take instant photos of the crime scene but will follow up with more detailed photos afterward.

A cartridge casing is the holding unit (typically brass, steel, or nickel) that contains the gunpowder, bullet, and primer.

J. Edgar Hoover is the first person to use the phrase "sexual predator."

Maggot eggs on a decedent indicates the victim has been dead for approximately one day.

DNA stands for deoxyribonucleic acid.

Fourier Transform Infrared (FTIR) spectrometry ascertains paint type from the way components will absorb infrared light.

Most serial killers begin to show their homicidal leanings during puberty.

Approximately twenty percent of gunshot exit wounds have microscopic gunshot residue.

On a crime scene, no one is allowed to turn lights on or off, turn water on or off, or use the toilet.

At death, maggots concentrate on the head and any open wounds.

According to research, serial killers never develop a sense of acceptance or being part of everyday life as most people do.

High velocity blood spatter is indicative of gunshot wounds and typically travels at a rate of more than one hundred feet per second.

Most arsonists have little or no self-confidence.

A bullet primer may consist of antimony, lead, and barium.

Regarding explosive forensics, a base charge is the primary explosive charge found inside a blasting cap.

The cannibal, Joe Metheny, would use the flesh of his victims and mix it with animal meat for sale to his customers in hamburgers.

Once asked why he didn't eat the victims he and Ottis Toole murdered, Henry Lucas said, "I don't like barbecue sauce."

Blood Pattern Analysis can determine the date and time of the crime as well as whether the suspect was right handed or left handed.

According to studies, serial killers were more abused as children than the general population with half being exposed to psychological abuse.

The tiny blank spots on the ridges of a fingerprint are skin pores.

A bullet that has ricocheted will collect trace evidence from the impact of the ricochet.

H. H. Holmes sold some of the skeletons of his victims of his murders to medical schools.

The skull sutures are useful in determining the age of the deceased.

Paint is composed of three major components:
1. Solvents
2. Binders
3. Pigments

Handgun bullet chamber pressure is typically 30,000 to 40,000 pounds per square inch.

Fingerprints on a human begin to develop at the three month mark in the womb.

Blood pattern transfer occurs when an object, wet with blood, comes in contact with another object.

Serial killer, Robert Pickton, would grind up the bodies of his victims and then feed the grindings to the pigs on his farm.

The human oral cavity harbors approximately 40,000 bacteria.

Notorious serial killer, Ed Gein, would go out at night and dig up the bodies of women. He made a female 'suit' and said he wanted to be a female.

The most common trace evidence is hair, fibers, glass, and paint.

Ted Bundy was a peeping Tom when he was a teen.

At any given time, there are approximately forty million working prostitutes.

When there is blood spatter and there is an area in that splatter that is missing spatter because of an object that was in the way is called a Void.

Jeffrey Dahmer used to give his neighbors in his apartment building sandwiches. It is rumored some of these sandwiches were made from some of his victims.

Regarding projectile penetration of glass on a crime scene, there are radial fractures (similar to the spokes of a bicycle) and concentric fractures that are arched fractures that connect the radial fractures.

Plastic Explosive is another name for PBX.

Transient evidence is that evidence that is temporary.

Transient evidence includes imprints in snow or mud, temperature, and odors.

There are warning signs as early as three years of age indicating that a child may grow up with criminal tendencies.

Contrary to popular belief, most robberies do not occur at banks, they occur on the streets and are robberies of people.

Bank robberies only account for approximately two percent of all robberies.

Over two million left-handed people are killed each year from mishandling equipment designed for right-handed individuals.

Because of the 'CSI Effect' many trial lawyers are having to spend time educating jurors on the reality of forensic evidence.

Only one crime scene investigator will sketch the crime scene.

Fibers are categorized as either natural, synthetic, and manufactured.

Blood will form an almost perfect spherical shape when it leaves the body.

Approximately eighty percent of human trafficking involves sex.

If a bullet passes through plastic, wood, glass, or fabric, each of these materials can leave small fragments and marks on the bullet.

When someone alters the crime scene intentionally to attempt to sway the investigation, that is called Crime Scene Staging.

Ted Bundy once worked at a suicide hotline.

The brain is composed of numerous divisions. One of those divisions is the orbital cortex. Individuals with low activity in the orbital cortex typically show an increase of sex, violence, drinking, and rage.

A traffic investigator can use skid marks to determine the speed of a vehicle before braking began.

The Zodiac Killer case file remains open.

The higher an organ's specific gravity, the greater the damage.

Mass shooting occur more often in businesses (approximately thirty-seven percent). Schools come in second at approximately thirty-four percent.

Where did the force originate that shattered a pane of glass?
1. Find the radial cracks.
2. Locate conchoidal lines on the edge.
3. Determine which side of the glass these lines generate right angles.
4. Once this is known, the examiner knows that the force originated from the opposite side.

The skin prints on the feet are as unique as fingerprints. Police will often take photos of the crowds at a crime scene because the suspect is sometimes likely to be hanging around.

An inchoate offense is the act of preparing to commit another crime.

Once damaged, a tooth cannot repair itself.

The first shot into plate glass will extend radial fractures in an unbroken pattern.

Subsequent shots into plate glass will have radial stopping points at the crossing of a previous shot's radial fracture.

Conditional evidence is that evidence produced by an event or action.

Bullets fired at close range can show a wide area of powder stippling but will lack muzzle imprints and lacerations.

Sometimes criminals will wear gloves to keep from leaving fingerprints. However, gloves can also leave imprints that are just as unique and individual as fingerprints.

Jeffrey Dahmer played with dead animals when he was a child.

When analyzing a bullet shot from a firearm, the forensic expert will look at lands and grooves that leave impressions on that bullet. A groove is the raised portion of the bullet (the milled out portion of the barrel portion of the firearm).

The angle at which blood hits a particular surface is called Angle of Impact.

Studying the ground surface looking for locations that potentially have buried objects is called forensic geomorphology.

John Wayne Gacy once crawled into the casket of a young man.

Most robbery offenders are male (approximately 96 percent).

Patent fingerprints are prints that can be seen with the naked eye.

Latent fingerprints require dusting or other procedures to be seen.

Exemplar prints are prints that have already been processed by police.

A approximately 1,500 feet per second a bullet becomes spherical.

The serial killer H. H. Holmes had a medical doctorate degree.

A forensics expert can determine the sequence of shots fired through glass by the shot's radial fracture stopping points.

Unlike the unrealistic representation on television and movies, it takes weeks to months to get results back on DNA.

Ted Bundy would fake an injury to lure his victims.

Evidence at a crime scene is not gathered until the crime scene has been diagramed, photographed, and all evidence is listed and referenced.

A suspect who is lying to you may change the pronouns in his language.

As a bullet leaves the body it will take blood with it and in the same direction of the bullet. This is called forward spatter.

Since 1900, Asian and Native American serial killers represent approximately 1.4 percent of all killings.

Half of all human trafficking involves children.

The aorta is approximately the size of a standard size watering hose.

Handwriting analysis is the area of questioned documents.

The diameter of a blood drop increases with the distance from which it dropped.

The body of Aileen Wuornos's last victim was never found.

The Zodiac Killer has never been caught.

In average, a human produces from three to nine ounces of feces each day.

Most suicides by a handgun are from a gunshot wound to the right temple area.

Most suicides from a shotgun are from a gun shot wound to the mouth.

Most suicides from a rifle are from a gunshot wound to the forehead.

Cast-off bloodstains happen when blood is thrown onto some surface from an object which has blood on it.

Crime scenes typically reflect the personality of the criminal.

People lie more in writing than face to face.

Most serial killers stated by acting on their desires on animals.

Only five to ten percent of crime scenes have evidence that can be used by detectives and forensics personnel.

Maggot pupae on a decedent indicates the victim has been dead for approximately eighteen to twenty-five days.

The serial killer, Lonnie Franklin (The Grim Sleeper) had a gap of thirteen years between murders.

A detective may interview a witness on a crime scene to determine if (s)he has information, but will do the formal interview at the police station.

Direction of force of broken glass can be determined by concentric and radial cracks.

Richard Ramirez was a self-confessed devil worshipper. A transfer blood pattern is where blood is left on a surface after having been left from another object such as a shoe.

Most serial killers do not kill outside their race.

Sometimes handwriting analysis is performed on graffiti.

The parts of a firearms that leave marks on bullets and casings are

1. Breach face
2. Firing pin
3. Firing chamber
4. Rifling
5. Ejector
6. Extractor

Each gun barrel is unique in its own way and produces a fired bullet with unique characteristics.

It is possible to create fake DNA in a lab.

Psychopaths have a greater fear threshold.

Jeffrey Dahmer used to collect road kill.

There are approximately 400,000 individuals in the United States who are registered sex offenders.

Males have approximately five to six liters of blood in their bodies.

Only 0.1 percent of DNA is different from everyone else. In other words, 99.9 percent of DNA is the same in everyone.

Fingerprints on firearms are recovered by using cyanoacrylate (super glue) fuming.

Roughly fifteen percent of serial killer victims are selected at random.

The heart of a human can pump blood forcefully enough to cause it to squirt as much as thirty feet away.

The mandible is the hardest bone in the human body.

H. H. Holmes is regarded as America's first serial killer with a confession of killing twenty-seven individuals.

The second most occurring purpose for human trafficking is forced labor.

The epidermis on a human replaces itself approximately every twenty-eight days.

Ted Bundy was a Boy Scout and law student.

Most robberies occur after 8:00 p.m. and before 3:00 a.m.

The transfer of trace evidence from one object to another object is called primary transfer.

that, each type of tape can vary with the same manufacturer and within the same batch of tape!

The FBI maintains a database of over 46,000 automotive paint samples from various manufacturers.

The ulnar loop is the most common fingerprint pattern in the United States.

A bullet reaching around 800 to 1,000 feet per second will realize a minor flattening of its nose.

Under normal conditions, if a deceased is warm and stiff, the approximate time of death is from three to eight hours previous.

A human can only survive for under thirty minutes in water that is 40 degrees Fahrenheit.

Former FBI agent Robert Ressler is the person who is given credit for first using the term "Serial Killer."
Human trafficking is not just for sex and labor, but also occurs for organ harvesting.

A binary explosive is composed to two materials that will not react (explode) until they are mixed together.

ignite. When this happens, the sweat that was transferred to the bullet casing immediately vaporizes and the trace salt residue melts and causes a chemical reaction with the casing and causes the fingerprint to be etched into the casing...permanently.

Back splatter is the blood spatter that comes back toward the gun after it is fired.

There are four types of fingerprints:
1. Tent
2. Whorl
3. Arch
4. Loop.

There are two basic types of blood stain patterns: passive and dynamic.

If one identical twin has a missing tooth during tooth development the other will also be missing the same tooth.

Moths appear on a deceased body at the end of the decomposition.

Duct tape is manufactured utilizing as many as fifty chemicals and each manufacturer's use can vary. Not only

Jeffrey Dahmer was killed in prison by an inmate who said the reason he killed him was that he kept molding his food into the shapes of human bones.

Maggots can eat approximately sixty percent of a human body in about seven days.

Factors that lessen the degree of guilt are called Mitigating Circumstances.

Bullets fired at a distance will typically have no powder indications and will leave a hole close to the size caliber of the bullet.

Iris scanning for the purpose of identification is ten times more accurate than fingerprinting.

By using blood spatter, a detective or forensics expert can often times tell where a victim was located when the injury was received.

Bullet fingerprints are often overlooked by suspects. When a bullet is loaded into a gun by hand a small amount of sweat (including trace amounts of salt) are transferred to the bullet casing. When the bullet is fired from the gun an immense amount of heat is created as the primer and gunpowder

Adermatoglyphia: the absence of ridges on the skin on the pads of the fingers and toes, as well as on the palms of the hands and soles of the feet.

A striation on a bullet are the microscopic marks on the fired bullet made from the firing from a gun.

Maggot larvae that is approximately five millimeters on a decedent indicates the victim has been dead for approximately one to two days.

Some individuals have two sets of DNA.

The reason bullets leave larger exit wounds than entry wounds is because the bullet expands and/or tumbles.

Transfer evidence is evidence that is produced by contact of one object against another.

There are differences between hair found from different parts of a person's body and even between hair found in the same region of a person's body.

At the approximate age of fifty the human brain begins to shrink.

Glass is classified as an amorphous solid.

Because glass is mass produced, it is considered class evidence.

Most bullets never hit their intended target. Only approximately ten percent of bullets fired by suspects hit their target.

Sometimes, when a body has been in the water for an extended period of time, the epidermis separates from the dermis. A fingerprint expert may cut the epidermis off of the body and put it on his hand like a glove in an effort to get fingerprints.

The serial killer, Ed Gein, boarded up most of the rooms in the home she spent her time in.

Shotgun wadding is unlikely to travel over twenty yards when fired.

Males between the ages of 34 and 44 are the most frequent customers of prostitutes.

The study of spores and pollen is called forensic palynology.

John Wayne Gacy's last words were, "Kiss my ass."

Specific markings made by a firearm when it is fired help forensics experts identify the make and model of the firearm used in the crime.

Blackmarket body parts. A broker will contact a funeral home to solicit the purchase of body parts. When the broker is successful, the parts are taken from the deceased and the body is sewn back together or cremated to hide the theft.

Dehydration causes death in about one week.

An individual's irides are unique.

Typically, larger caliber firearms leave more reproducible markings than smaller calibers.

Filing off a serial number on a gun does not eliminate the gun's serial number. When the serial number is stamped on the gun, the underlying metal is compressed and that compression leaves the serial number impression deep in the metal.

A blood saturation pattern occurs when blood has been absorbed into materials such as clothing and carpet.

A bullet fired from a gun can be split by striking bone.

Forensic experts can ascertain what type of glass is found at a crime scene based on the color and composition, For instance, the glass used for a drinking glass has a different composition than that used in the glass of a motor vehicle.

Jeffrey Dahmer was nicknamed "The Milwaukee Cannibal" and "The Milwaukee Monster."

When an arsonist sets a public building on fire it is typically set in a building's public bathroom.

Pentaerythritoltetranitrate is a multi-use high explosive.

Firearms evidence as small as a fragment of a bullet can provide information on the type of firearm used.

Dental imprints are as individualistic as fingerprints.

Gunpowder additives can include plasticizers, coolant, flash inhibitors, and stabilizers.

Approximately seventy percent of people believe there is nothing wrong with pirating downloads online.

Twenty percent of children have been solicited for sex online.

Medium velocity blood spatter is typically representative of blunt force or arterial spray and is typically at a velocity of five to one hundred feet per second.

Only about ten percent of all crimes are reported to police.

Bullet entry wounds into the skull usually produces a coning (bevel) of the bone surface.

Maggots on a deceased body can be processed to analyze poisons that may have been in the victim prior to death.

Most arsonists set fire to the target structure outside.

Brass cartridges retain fingerprints better than cartridges made from nickle materials.

The biggest problem with analyzing bullet evidence is the condition of the evidence.

Indented impressions (impressions made on paper beneath the original copy) have been successfully recovered from as far down as seven layers.

Most sexual predators have victims who are the same race as they are.

Cast-off blood spatter represents blood that was swung through the air.

A jacketed bullet will typically shed its copper jacket in the subcutaneous tissue of the subject while the bullet will proceed along its path.

Serial killer, Richard Ramirez, got married while on death row.

DNA evidence must be placed in paper bags because when it is placed in plastic bags it can damage or destroy the DNA.

Tear wounds (lacerations) have low to medium velocity blood spatter.

The word *forensic derives* from the Latin word "forensis," which means "of or before the forum" (before the court).

Floater: Corpse located in water.

Approximately eighty percent of La Cosa Nostra members live in New York City.

Most arsonists are male.

Some brands of cigarettes have manufacturing numbers printed on them.

Most suicides are gunshots to the head.

A hair from a female is approximately half the diameter of that of a male.

Pollen on a suspect's car or clothing can place him or her on a crime scene.

In the United States arsonists set more than half a million fires every year.

Fibers can remain intact for years.

Almost all bullets are manufactured to not exit the body.

A bullet fired from a distance and entering in individual usually leaves an entry wound close to the caliber of the bullet.

For evidentiary purposes, both the rough sketch and the final, finished sketch are 'discoverable.'

In handwriting analysis, requested specimens are those writings that are dictated to the writer by the investigator.

William Kemmlar is the first person to be executed by the electric chair.

A comparison microscope is the tool used to compare bullet and/or cartridge cases.

Iris scans are the most accurate type of biometric identification.

If a piece of trace evidence seems important and will be utilized in further testing, the trace evidence is called probative.

Frangible bullets are typically made of powdered copper.

There are three types of firing pin impressions:
1. Extractor marks
2. Breech marks
3. Ejector marks

No change in shape of a bullet occurs until it reached a velocity of approximately 800 feet per second.

Hair is a very common trace evidence item found on a crime scene.

Negative pressure upon a bullet entering a body creates brief cavitation and can pull skin into the wound.

Indirect evidence does not prove or disprove a material question of fact.

A velocity of approximately 200 feet per second is required to penetrate skin and bone.

Approximately four percent of robberies resulted in the loss of over $250,000 each.

The human skull is composed of twenty-nine different bones.

Gunpowder burns at different rates:
1. Depressive – as it burns the burning surface area decreases.
2. Neutral – burn is a constant speed.
3. Progressive – as it burns the burning surface area increases.

A Munsell Chart is used to color grade soil evidence.

Circumstantial evidence is evidence that is founded on suggestion.

The skull of a skeleton can tell detectives the sex of the deceased.

Bullets produced in some parts of Europe and in the Middle East may be manufactured with primers that contain mercury.

The sciatic notch is wider in females than in males, an indicator of sex to forensic anthropologists.

The Italian La Cosa Nostra generates approximately $500 billion in revenue each year.

Class evidence is that evidence that can be classed with a group of things that share given properties.

The International Ink Library maintains a database of more than 9,500 inks that have been produced since the 1920s.

Human trafficking is one of the fastest growing crimes.

Serial killer Charles Comer's last words were, "Go Raiders!"

Rigor mortis lasts about thirty-six hours.

Maggot pre-pupae on a decedent indicates the victim has been dead for approximately seven to twelve days.

Shotgun wadding from a shotgun shell can be used to determine such information as the shotgun manufacturer and the gauge of the shotgun.

When meeting someone new, the average person will tell two or three lies in the first ten minutes.

The CSI Effect: Jurors on a case expecting to see the unrealistic results they see on television.

Retinal identification is based on the individual's unique blood vessels on the back of the eye.

If a bullet does not hit bone and lodges in only soft tissue may be relatively intact.

After committing a murder, most serial killers experience a sense of relief.

Cranial morphology is one of the best determinants of the race of a skeleton.

A majority of counterfeiters are male (approximately seventy-nine percent).

Arsenic detection in corpses was developed in 1773 by Carl Scheele.

Before fingerprinting, police used a technique called Bertillionage created by Alphonse Bertillon that used the uniqueness of the proportions of the human body as identification.

In order to properly compare a hair, a forensics expert needs about twenty-five to fifty control samples.

Revolvers and pistols are not the same. A revolver typically refers to a handgun with a revolving cylinder that holds the gun's cartridges.

Organized serial killers typically respond more favorably when interviewed using questioning that is direct and to the point.

Each human tongue print is unique.

Human trafficking produces a profit of approximately $32,000,000,000 each year.

The Angle of Convergence in blood spatter evidence is that area that contains the intersections of the angles of the blood spatter from the area where the blood spatter is located into the surrounding spatial area.

If used in a poisoning homicide, cyanide leaves a scent of almonds in the deceased's body.

Ted Bundy was finally identified because of a bite mark he left on the butt of one of his victims.

Many serial killers will keep some type of souvenir of their crime.

Homicide detectives can estimate a time of death by measuring the amount of livor mortis in the decedent's body.

Jeffrey Dahmer is purported to have had a significant behavior change after hernia surgery when he was six years of age.

There is an act called 'blood farming' where people are held against their will and their blood is removed and sold in the black market.

TNT is short for trinitrotoluene.

Most sex offenders are between twenty-five and sixty-five years of age.

When green spots develop on a dead body it is because of enzymes in the organs digesting themselves.

In a bullet, gunpowder stabilizers can include methyl centralite, diphenylamine, and ethyl centralite.

There is a 0.7 percent chance any given person will die from a homicide.

Most crime scene evidence is contaminated.

Canine evidence is not admissible in the courts but it gives detectives a place to start.

Iris identification was originally proposed by Frank Birch in 1936.

Serial killers typically grow up without friends and isolated.

The pooling of blood inside a deceased person is called livor mortis.

The brain is approximately 80 percent water.

There are many possible materials that can make up soil:

1. Minerals
2. Rock
3. Pollen
4. Vegetation decomposition
5. Animal particulate (decomposition and excretory)
6. Pollutants and contaminants

Approximately seventy-five percent of kids who are solicited online do not tell their parents.

Most suicides are committed with a revolver.

Vehicle manufacturers conduct tests on their vehicles that provide crash data that traffic accident investigators can use to determine a particular vehicle's speed. These tests include information on depth of crush so that an investigator can measure the actual crush of a vehicle and take the test crash information to determine that speed.

The markings on a bullet after fired can help detectives determine the make and model of gun used.

Consciousness is lost when a person reaches 15,000 feet altitude.

Natural fibers are produced by nature and have rough edges with an uneven appearance. Man-made (synthetic) fibers are smooth.

A pair of eyeballs are worth $1,500 (approximately).

The average age of robbery offenders is thirty-three years.

A silencer used on a gun may generate non-typical wounds upon entry.

Gunshot residue can consist of gunpowder (unburned and burned), primer particulate (unburned or burned), lubricants that may have been used to clean the gun, bullet surface particulate, and cartridge casing particulate.

When a forensics expert matches two objects as having been part of one piece, that is called a fracture match.

Humans are born with 300 bones. When reaching adult age, the human body has 206 bones.

Under normal conditions, a human body decreases in temperature 1.6 degrees per hour until it reaches environment temperature. This is called algor mortis or the Death Chill.

Most burglaries occur during the daytime.

A liar will typically repeat your question in their answer.

The iris of the eye is colored based on the amount of melatonin pigment present.

A bullet is the projectile that is shot from the gun when it fires.

Panic can cause witnesses to remember things differently than they actually happened.

Liquid chromatography can be used to identify the chemical composition of inks used in writing.

Sixty percent of people lie at least once in a ten minute conversation.

Bullet wounds can reveal information regarding the distance from which the subject was shot, caliber, type of bullet used, sequence of hits, and bullet velocity.

Serial killer, Albert Fish, used to stick needles into his scrotum and butt so he could enjoy the pain.

Maggot larvae that is approximately ten millimeters on a decedent indicates the victim has been dead for approximately two to three days.

Up to 800,000 people are trafficked each year and eighty percent are female.

A victim who has removed clothing from the wound area prior to the shot indicates that the death was probably a suicide.

A preponderance of serial killers were abused as children.

Disorganized serial killers typically return to the crime scene to relive their murder.

Females have approximately four to five liters of blood in their bodies.

Dental records are responsible for identifying approximately 93 percent of victims.

By using various measurements on the human skull, forensic anthropologists can determine the race (ancestry) of a skeletal victim.

Only approximately fourteen percent of all burglaries are solved.

The skeleton represents fourteen percent of a body's weight.

Gunshot residue distribution is influenced by the type of weapon used to fire the bullet.

Psychopaths represent approximately one percent of the total population.

There are more lies told over the telephone than by any other means.

How is an autopsy performed?
1. The chest is opened through a 'Y' incision. The cut is made from the shoulders to the sternum.
2. Major organs are taken out and then weighed.
3. The stomach is analyzed and can be used to estimate time of death by the amount of digestion of food.
4. The skull is then opened and the brain taken out.
5. Organs are placed back inside the body and is sewn back together.

A preponderance of shootings involving handguns occur less than seven yards away.

A person's fingernails grow 400 percent faster than toenails.

Jeffrey Dahmer once stole a store mannequin and kept it for his sexual needs.

Approximately seven percent of humans are left-handed.

Deleted computer files may not delete from your computer and can stay there until it is rewritten.

Canines used to find decomposing bodies are trained using a synthetic chemical that simulates the scent of a decaying body.

Shotgun pellets, when fired, may become deformed simply from the firing of the shell.

A typical square inch of the skin on a human is home for approximately thirty-two million bacteria.

Revolvers and pistols are not the same. A pistol typically refers to a semi-automatic handgun.

An individual's eyes are different from each other.

Organized serial killers typically dismember their victims.

Drug trafficking offenders receive an average of five and one-half years incarceration.

The color and physical structure of the eye is linked to genetics but the intricate details of the patterns are not genetically linked.

A triple base explosive contains nitroglycerine, nitrocellulose, and nitroguanidine.

Forensic anthropologists typically use the teeth of a skeleton to determine the age of a child victim but use bone osteons and arthritis to determine the age of an adult.

The DNA of identical twins is the same but the fingerprints are still unique to each individual.

Organized serial killers typically will contact police as a taunting factor.

Autopsies can now be performed digitally without cutting the body into pieces.

Approximately eighty percent of those in sexual slavery are age twenty-three and under.

There are approximately 2,500,000 home burglaries / invasions each year.

Most liars will speak using words without contractions.

On the black market one can purchase blood, various body parts, and even bones.

Forensic Entomology is the field of science that studies insects at crime scenes.

Indented impressions (impressions made on paper beneath the original copy) have been successfully recovered from as far back in time as sixty years.

Some of the best trace evidence is glitter. There are only a handful of glitter manufacturers across the world and each uses their own shapes, refractions, and thicknesses. These various properties are retained in a database and can be matched against any glitter evidence found on a crime scene. Glitter is extremely hard to wipe off.

A serial killer who kills spontaneously is typically classified as a Disorganized Killer.

Eyewitness evidence is preferred over forensic evidence.

Most home burglaries occur in July and August.

The human brain uses 20 percent of the oxygen that enters the blood.

Under normal conditions, if a deceased is cold and not stiff, the approximate time of death is eight to thirty-six hours previous.

DNA evidence is not 100 percent accurate as humans can make mistakes.

Gunshot wounds are usually categorized in one of three types:
1. Contact
2. Intermediate range
3. Distant range

Human bodies give off sulphur and ammonia after death.

"Lockard's Principle of Exchange," the foundation of criminal forensics, states every criminal will bring something to the crime scene and take something away from it.

A cartridge is the whole, unfired round of ammo.

Jeffrey Dahmer was discharged from the United States Army for alcoholism.

Over ninety-five percent of mass shooters had mental health issues.

Luminol can destroy the evidence it identifies.

Approximately fifteen percent of all robberies were conducted by career offenders.

The average person loses between 50 to 100 strands of hair each day.

When Ed Gein was a teenager, he would often babysit with children.

Each gun has its own groves and lands (a gun's fingerprint) that are unique to that gun.

The Father of Forensics is Edmond Locard who was influenced by Sherlock Holmes.

Paint samples as tiny as 1/32 of an inch square is all that is needed for forensic paint testing.

A Forensic Science Technician is responsible for obtaining, classifying, and then analyzing the physical evidence taken from the crime scene.

Approximately ninety-five percent of sexual offenders know their victim.

The pelvis of a skeleton can tell detectives the sex of the victim.

Rigor mortis is caused from the calcium build up in the muscles.

Hair from a human is very strong and almost indestructible.

Forensic Psychologists adjoin psychological applications to the criminal justice system.

Disorganized serial killers typically do not dismember their victims.

Low velocity blood spatter is typically dripping blood and travels at the rate of five feet per second or less.

A person who has lost approximately one and a half liters of blood may lose consciousness.

Fracture lines in dense bone such as skulls can identify distance, velocity and direction of fire.

Bullet comparison involves both class and individual indicators.
1. Class: rifling and caliber type.
2. Individual: used to attempt to identify a particular firearm.

The first book documenting forensic procedures was written in the 13th century entitled, "The Washing Away of Wrongs."

Just because someone has marked over something they have written does not make the original writing unrecoverable.

Refractive index and birefringence are optical qualities used to analyze synthetic fibers.

A Parent Stain (blood) is a blood stain from which a satellite stain began.

Maggot larvae that is approximately sixteen to seventeen millimeters on a decedent indicates the victim has been dead for approximately four to five days.

Forensic psychologists can oftentimes look at a homicide crime scene and determine a profile of the murder suspect simply from that crime scene.

The 'glow' of luminol lasts only approximately thirty seconds.

Forensic Taphonomy is the study of how organisms decay and fossilize.

The science of forensics wasn't begun with scientist, but with police officers.

Disorganized serial killers respond more favorable to interviews using counseling techniques.

Shockwaves from a bullet compress the skin and tissue for a short few milliseconds prior to hitting the target.

Approximately half of all drug traffickers had no prior criminal history.

Bullet markings are not easily matched.

Beveling around an entrance wound holds clues.

Everything you do online can be traced.

Bullets do not usually transverse a straight line to the target, they typically have yaw, nutation, and precession.

Using various wavelength radiation, it is possible with a Video Spectral Comparator (VSC) to read through covered writings made from a different ink.

An Electrostatic Detection Apparatus (ESDA) is used to identify writing impressions on paper below the original writing.

Serial killers who hide the body and weapon are classified as Organized Killers.

Luminol is composed of hydrogen, nitrogen, carbon, and oxygen and turns blue when it comes in contact with blood.

The United States has the highest prison population.

An estimated $6 million is generated in profits from stolen body parts each year.

Semen has the highest concentration of DNA.

The first evidence of insects being used to assist in crime solving was in China in the 1240s.

The firing pins of guns leave impressions on the bullet casing or primer when the gun is fired. The impression made by the firing pin is often unique...even between different guns of the same make and model.

Koala bears have fingerprints so close to humans it is difficult for experts to tell them apart.

Under normal conditions, if a deceased is cold and stiff, the approximate time of death is over thirty-six hours previous.

Using maggots, entomologists can determine with reasonable certainty the general time a decedent was killed or dumped.

Detectives have to be careful when using luminol to detect blood on a crime scene as it also reacts with copper, urine, and horseradish sauce.

A liver is worth $160,000 (approximately).

In the seconds after death, your brain has a surge in activity.

Even if an arm or leg of a victim is cut off, some of the ink from a tattoo on that appendage can be found in the victim's lymph nodes.

Most police calls are not criminal in nature, but civil.

Hair has the lowest concentration of DNA.

Up to 17,000 people are trafficked in the United States annually.

Crime typically increases during a full moon.

Identical twins have different iris patterns.

Deposits of gun residue can land on individuals who are in close proximity to the firearm discharge and not just on the person holding the gun.

Other Works
by this
Author

How to Catch a Liar
Indicators to help determine if someone is lying to you.
Some of the same techniques used by police detectives.

Outside Your Door
A compendium of true crime and police stories from the
police career of Steven David Lampley.

Serial Killer
(Inside the Mind of a Serial Killer)
A different approach to why serial killers do what they do.

www.StevenDavidLampley.com

Copyright © 2017 by Steven David Lampley

All rights reserved. No part of this publication may be reproduced, distributed, or transmitted in any form or by any means, including photocopying, recording, or other electronic or mechanical methods, without the prior written permission of the publisher, except in the case of brief quotations embodied in critical reviews and certain other noncommercial uses permitted by copyright law.

For permission requests: StevenDavidLampley.com.

Printed in the United States of America

Oliphant Publishing

First Printing, 2017

ISBN-13: 978-1975602543

ISBN-10: 1975602544

www.StevenDavidLampley.com

DEDICATED TO MY SONS

Christopher Brenton Lampley
Michael Brandon Lampley
Jason Andrew Lampley

Steven David Lampley

"STEVEN IS QUITE THE STORYTELLER.
HE HAS A TALENT FOR WRITING, FILLING
THE READER WITH EMOTION. YOU'LL
LEAVE INSPIRED. GET READY
FOR THE RIDE."
~Marlena Smith
(The Life I Live)

"I AM BLOWN AWAY."
~Marlena Smith
The Life I Live)

"SOME REALLY AWESOME BOOKS!"
~Tessa Mauro
(Talk Show Host)

"I LITERALLY CRIED HARDER THAN
I HAVE AT SOME FUNERALS AND I
LAUGHED HARDER THAN I HAVE AT
COMEDY SHOWS. DEFINATELY A ROLLER
COASTER OF EMOTIONS AND I
LOVED EVERY MOMENT."
~Ember Hammond
(Co-Host, Color Me Dead Podcast)

"MEET A MOST INCREDIBLE MAN.
HE'S LIKE SHERLOCK HOLMES AND
'LIE TO ME' ALL IN ONE:
DETECTIVE AND AUTHOR"
~Anne Terri
(Writer/Director)

"I READ 'OUTSIDE YOUR DOOR' AND
COULD NOT STOP UNTIL FINISHING.
YOU HAVE HAD A VERY AWESOME,
INTERESTING LIFE. I PLAN TO
READ THEM ALL."
~Shirley Johnson
(Legal Secretary, Former Court Reporter)

WHAT PEOPLE ARE SAYING

"POLICE OFFICER TO POLICE OFFICER,
YOU'RE AT LEGEND STATUS!"
~Ryan Patterson
(Law Enforcement)

"HIS SKILLS PLACE HIM IN THE
'CREAM OF THE CROP' CATEGORY."
~William T. Gaut, PhD.
(Former Deputy Chief, Homicide Division)

"STEVEN LAMPLEY DOES A MASTERFUL
JOB OF, NOT ONLY TAKING US ONTO THE
BEAT AND STREETS WITH HIM, BUT FINDING
GEMS OF LIFE-TRUTHS THAT WE CAN TAKE
AWAY FROM HIS WAR STORIES.
MAY ALL OF US LEARN THEM WELL."
~Troy King
(Alabama Attorney General – 2006-2011)